FEMININE MASCULINE BALANCE

BLENDING SOME FEMININE AND MASCULINE PRINCIPLES

FEMININE	BALANCE	MASCULINE
Cyclical	Spiral	Linear
Intuitive	Sensible	Rational
Emotional	Aware	Logical
Imaginative/Poetic	Knowing	Analytical/"Intellectual"
Holistic/Inclusive	Integrative	Hierarchical/Divisive
Reflective	Proactive	Reactive
Providing/Sustaining	Nurturing	Protective/Defensive
Amenable	Collaborative	Competitive
Dependent	Interdependent	Independent
Being—In the flow	Mindfulness/Coherence—In action	Doing—Action-orientated
Sensitive	Compassionate	Detached (Indifferent)
Weak	Flexible	Strong
Allowing others to control their own lives	Trusting	Controlling one's own life
Receptive (Receiving)	Responsive	Outgoing (Giving)
(Produces) Quality	Discerning	(Produces) Quantity

Feminine Masculine Balance

A PARADIGM SHIFT FOR A PEACEFUL AND ABUNDANT SOCIETY

Jacqueline Mcleod

LIONCREST
PUBLISHING

FEMININE MASCULINE BALANCE

A Paradigm Shift for a Peaceful and Abundant Society

ISBN   978-1-5445-1156-6 *Paperback*

978-1-5445-1155-9 *Ebook*

To my wonderful children, Matthew and Johanna,
their partners, Maria and Josh,
current grandchildren, Romeo and Cassandra,
and any future grandchildren.
May Feminine Masculine Balance be achieved in your lifetime!

Contents

Preface

It's been a long time coming, but 2017 tipped open a global outpouring for change, exposing some of the most insidious elements of the patriarchy to public examination.

Groundswell movements like the Women's March, Black Lives Matter, #timesup, and the National School Walkouts for gun control raised a universal call against violence and domination. We are poised on a paradigm shift, but at its core, this is beyond gender, race, or politics.

Underneath the layers of misogyny, entitlement, and exploitation lies a profound imbalance between the value and expression of masculine qualities over the feminine— and Jacqueline McLeod nails it at its source. Her aim is not to overthrow the patriarchy but to heal and balance it. In *Feminine Masculine Balance*, Jacqueline tackles the big picture with extraordinary clarity, drawing on both research and personal experience to explain how feminine and masculine aspects are present in all individuals, but living 6,000 years under a patriarchy has created a damaged society with devalued feminine qualities and a pumped-up, out-of-balance masculine. It affects our relationships, our safety, our health, and our potential on all levels.

Feminine Masculine Balance examines ways to shift perspective and balance feminine and masculine aspects, giving a language and vision for a more peaceful future. Jacqueline dismantles limited gender and societal roles and expectations with a practical, considered approach based on non-violence, equality, and acceptance. Feminine and masculine qualities (equal but different) are brought together to become a powerful agent for growth and opportunity. This is not only a wonderful and inspiring revelation but an incredibly useful hands-on guide to living and communicating with respect and harmony.

MERRYL KEY
Holistic Health Practitioner
BA Communications
Dip Health Sciences
Dip Applied Astrology

Introducing Feminine Masculine Balance

A PARADIGM SHIFT

In this supposedly advanced, civilised age, each of us—regardless of our gender—is made up of both feminine and masculine energies or principles. Unfortunately, masculine energies have dominated society for millennia and, because feminine energies have traditionally been so devalued, we continue to feel stressed and struggle with confusion and chaos. It all comes back to balancing the feminine and masculine. What would happen if people finally woke up?

The intention of this book is to journey towards achieving Feminine Masculine Balance (FMB). This requires a paradigm shift, which is to acknowledge the evolution of our thinking and to take it a step further to the next level.

But first I will explain how my journey began.

THE SIDE EFFECTS OF WAR

Years ago, I read that there were societies in the Neolithic period that were female-centred, as opposed to female-ruled (*rulership* being a masculine-dominated term). Archaeological evidence shows that these villages had no fortifications—except those to protect against wild animals—no weapons, and no evidence of violence in the bodies found in gravesites. Presumably, people in these communities resolved conflict through peaceful means, and the society was relatively balanced in terms of the feminine and masculine.

Being a post-World War II baby, I grew up observing the ill effects of the war. A friend's father had been killed, and the lack of a father clearly had a sad effect on the boy. Another friend's father was seriously injured and, although the surgeons saved his legs, he was in constant pain. I was lucky. My father failed his medical examination and was unable to enlist. This pleased my mother; however, I suspect not enlisting also had an impact on his life.

If I had been a boy, I would have been in the ballot for the draft to fight in Vietnam. Fortunately, my brother was a year too old and none of my close friends were drafted. One of the boys in our faculty, who was a good actor, was called up for a medical examination. He arrived with an umbrella and a handbag, behaving in a very camp way, and he failed. Another fled the country, but that resulted in his family being hounded by the authorities. Another ridiculed the psychological testing and failed "due to chronic hay fever".

There was a drastic switch in just that one generation. Most men in my father's generation willingly went to war, thinking it was a grand adventure or at least their duty. Most men in my generation (at least the ones I knew) were vehemently opposed to war. Perhaps this was because of their fathers' experiences.

For years, I didn't watch TV, so I wasn't subjected to the horrors of war depicted on it but, nonetheless, I could never understand why it had to occur, and I was disgusted by any form of violence.

My upbringing, coupled with the discovery of the Neolithic communities, got me thinking:

- Is violence inevitable, as some people think?
- Isn't it obvious that violence breeds violence and war is futile?

- What if we could resolve disagreements in a non-violent way?
- To extend the concept, wouldn't a society balanced in the feminine and masculine help solve many other issues?

STUCK IN A RUT

For all the advancements in our modern age, for all the technological wonders, we still accept things as they are and never seem to learn from our mistakes.

A well-known quote, attributed to Edmund Burke, is, "Those who don't know history are destined to repeat it". It's like we are stuck in a rut.

Certainly, the world's problems are complicated. We can't fix everything with the snap of our fingers, but it should be obvious to everyone that things are out of balance. From climate change to economics, there's been a definite shift over the past few decades. Our solutions are mere bandages, and we're missing the very thing that lies beneath it all, that there are significant imbalances between feminine and masculine principles.

THE FEMININE AND MASCULINE

While studying astrology and tarot, I learned that masculine and feminine energies, or principles, have been recognised for eons, but I noticed that in our Masculine-Dominated Society (M-DS), feminine energies were often denigrated. Men used to refer to women's intuition in a very disparaging way. Curious, because they had gut feelings! They said, "Let's not get emotional", as if there were something wrong with emotions and, "Oh, it's just her imagination", as if imagination were a negative trait.

Many people mistakenly use the term *feminine* synonymously with women and *masculine* synonymously with men, and generally women embody and represent the feminine and men the masculine. To avoid this generality, some people instead choose to write about yin (feminine) and yang (masculine). These concepts are used within Taoism, and the yin and yang are considered to be two halves of a whole, or two sides of a coin. As you can see in the image, the yin and yang in the symbol are fused in a circle with a bit of each in the other.

However, if we use the terms *yin* and *yang*, not only are they foreign terms and people get confused with which is which, we are not addressing the problem that the feminine is considered synonymous with women and masculine with men. This masculine-dominated thinking is so deeply entrenched in us that it is quite a stretch for us to think otherwise. As with yin and yang, I think it is also important to look at these energies as two parts of a whole/two sides of a coin that need to be in balance, rather than the feminine and masculine being separate.

From these concepts, I wondered what would happen if the feminine energies were empowered to the same level as the masculine? What if they could be balanced? Instead of taking the feminine principle of **sensitivity** or the masculine principle of **detachment/indifference**, we could blend the two and have the principle of **compassion**. Instead of following the masculine principle of **controlling one's own life** or the feminine principle of **allowing others to control their own lives**, there could be **trust**. There are many examples of this type of balance. I selected some Feminine and Masculine principles and created the accompanying table, Blending Some Feminine and Masculine Principles, which will serve as a basis for the upcoming chapters and social situations discussed.

BLENDING SOME FEMININE AND MASCULINE PRINCIPLES

FEMININE	BALANCE	MASCULINE
Cyclical	Spiral	Linear
Intuitive	Sensible	Rational
Emotional	Aware	Logical
Imaginative/Poetic	Knowing	Analytical/"Intellectual"
Holistic/Inclusive	Integrative	Hierarchical/Divisive
Reflective	Proactive	Reactive
Providing/Sustaining	Nurturing	Protective/Defensive
Amenable	Collaborative	Competitive
Dependent	Interdependent	Independent
Being—In the flow	Mindfulness/Coherence—In action	Doing—Action-orientated
Sensitive	Compassionate	Detached (Indifferent)
Weak	Flexible	Strong
Allowing others to control their own lives	Trusting	Controlling one's own life
Receptive (Receiving)	Responsive	Outgoing (Giving)
(Produces) Quality	Discerning	(Produces) Quantity

At the end of this book is a copy of this table, which can be cut out to use as a reference as you read the book and also as a bookmark.

Another way to view this concept, in terms of symbols, is to consider a straight line (masculine), circle (feminine), and a spiral (balance).

A line has a beginning, middle, and end. It is unidirectional and works like an arrow, moving in one direction with focus, without breadth, and unable to move back on itself (lack of **reflection**).

A line is symbolic of the stories we tell, the way we have been educated, and the way we operate in the masculine-dominated world.

A circle has no beginning, middle, or end, and has breadth. It can have stages that repeat such as birth, growth, culmination, decay, death, birth, growth...

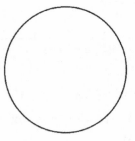

Circular energy is the way nature operates. The Earth cycles around the Sun, the Moon cycles around the Earth, the seasons follow in cycles, and day and night reappear in cycles. Traditionally, the Earth is described as feminine because so much about it is cyclical. The downside of the circle is that it can also represent a treadmill.

Combining the circle and the straight line produces a spiral, the masculine and feminine combined. It has length as well as breadth and width. It represents movement, change, and growth because, although it returns, it does not arrive at exactly the same place.

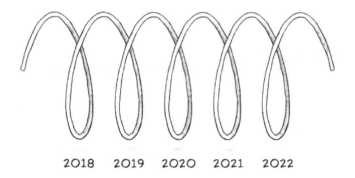

2018   2019   2020   2021   2022

For example, the spiral could represent years, patterns of behaviour, or life experiences. Someone can come back to the same point in their life having learned from the last cycle. They will have a better understanding of the issue the spiral represents.

On the other hand, if one is spiralling downwards, for example in the case of a drug addict, they would be returning to the same place, but worse off. Addiction (also discussed in Chapter 11) is a downward spiral in that it commences with someone using a drug to fill an emptiness while sometimes providing pleasure and relaxation. It feels like the drug makes life easier and provides a temporary reprieve from the stresses of life. As people use these substances more frequently, their lives start to deteriorate. It generally takes some time to realise it, but they are now trapped in this downward spiral, which, unless they manage to escape their addiction, leads to insanity or even death.

Spirals are one of the oldest symbols and can mean different things to different people and cultures.

FEMININE DOESN'T EQUAL WOMAN

As I mentioned before, society frequently uses the terms *feminine* and *women* synonymously and *men* and *masculine* synonymously. They are not synonymous. In general terms, men embody and represent the masculine energies and women embody and represent the feminine energies. Women tend to have more curved bodies and are generally more **intuitive, emotional,** and **imaginative.** Men tend to have more angular bodies and are generally more **rational, logical,** and **analytical.** In other words, in most cases, men have more masculine energy than feminine energy and women have more feminine energy than masculine energy, as symbolised in the yin-yang symbol. However, whether we have a masculine or feminine body, we express and operate with both energies.

To further help people understand this, there is a physical analogy: whether you are a man or a woman, you need progesterone (female hormone) and testosterone (male hormone) to have a healthy, functioning body.

This type of feminism or Feminine Masculine Balance (FMB) is described as empowering, respecting, and valuing the feminine in both men and women. It's not what most people consider feminism today—which I consider *womanism*, because it's focused on women, the very important issue of gender equality, etc. FMB is not meant to replace the other types of feminism but can complement them. I think it's a pity that some feminists see all men as the enemy because men who are in favour of gender equality can often be more effective in changing the minds of misogynists than women can. In valuing the feminine in women and men, we elevate, for example, being **intuitive, emotional**, and **imaginative** to be equally important as being **rational, logical**, and **analytical.** By respecting the feminine, we can find the balance in the two energies.

Women, representing the feminine, have been continually denigrated for centuries. One way women, and consequently the feminine, have been belittled is via language. In Dale Spender's book *Man Made Language*, she argues that "women have known for centuries that men have been the undeservedly dominant sex, and that their dominance is reflected and reinforced in language and by language use[1]". Some examples of masculine words compared to their feminine counterparts include: *hero/heroine* (these days, women are often referred to as heroes), *actor/actress* (sadly, many actresses call themselves actors for this reason), *bachelor/spinster* (*bachelorette* is now often used, -ette being a diminutive suffix), *sage/crone*, *dog/bitch*, *horse/nag*, *master/mistress* (my postgraduate degree is not called a Mistress of Science!).

A BREATH OF FRESH AIR

As I have indicated, this book is not a book about the usual forms of feminism, but it is a breath of fresh air and a way to move forward and *bridge the gap* between women and men. My business card states that I am a "free spirit", "independent scholar" and "joyful mother and grandmother". My goal is to bring these into the book for you.

A free spirit is a person who is true to themselves. They can be conventional, but they observe practices that feel right to them. For example, I chose to have home births because I was unimpressed with the way my friends had been treated in the hospital. Also, I became a vegetarian forty years ago, when very few people in Australia were vegetarian. It suited me and that's why I did it, not because

---

1   Dale Spender, *Man Made Language* (United Kingdom: Routledge and Kegan Paul, 1985), xii.

I wanted others to join me. I'm true to myself without expecting other people to follow me.

An independent scholar is one who develops wisdom via growth. I don't presume to be an expert on this topic in terms of qualifications from masculine-dominated educational institutions. Instead, I have developed my ideas through life experience and observation. I've travelled to many different countries and have done so with an open mind, such that I recognised immediately that most people want to live peacefully. The most important people in their lives are family. Wars and greed cause untold damage and we need to find ways to eliminate them.

THE DISTINCTION BETWEEN THE WORDS *MASCULINE* AND *MASCULINE-DOMINATED*

While reading this book, I want you to keep in mind the concepts are not constructively criticising men, rather they are constructively criticising the M-DS, which is made up of both men and women.

The masculine or masculine energies such as those in the table earlier are pure energy, neither "good" nor "bad". When used in a balanced way, the contribution to society is invaluable; however, when a number of masculine energies line up and are expressed without being balanced by feminine energies, they become distorted and dominating. The term *masculine-dominating* refers to these circumstances.

Similarly, feminine energies need to be balanced by masculine energies, and when they are not, extreme passivity, dependence, and lack of energy, initiative, and enthusiasm occurs. The feminine quality of lateral thinking can also become vague and erratic if not balanced with the masculine linear thinking, which directs the lateral ideas into a concrete outcome.

PUTTING IT INTO PRACTICE

This paradigm shift is vital and necessary, and we can only achieve this when we value and respect equally the feminine in both men and women. In the upcoming chapters, I will walk you through eleven social conditions where the masculine principles dominate a situation or area of life, and I will show you how balancing feminine energies with masculine energies can significantly change the outcome. For example, relationships between women and men would vastly improve and we would no longer lose our young men (and now women) to war. With the elimination of violence, there would no longer be refugees and the massive issues related to how to accommodate all their needs. Democracy would be improved, people would be less stressed, and there would be greater overall abundance.

By making the paradigm shift to FMB, we are able to move forward towards peace and abundance.

CHAPTER 1

Women and Men Are Different, Not Opposite

There are many social conditions that require this paradigm shift, but we're going to focus on eleven in this book. Let's get right into the first one.

As we discussed in the introduction, men and women are not alien creatures to one another. They have testosterone and progesterone, both of which are essential for a healthy, functioning body. That being said, they are also different.

AN UNCONVENTIONAL FAMILY

I grew up not being very aware that gender difference was a big deal, mostly because my mother "wore the pants" in the family. She was dominant and controlling, with a narcissistic personality disorder. My father was a quiet, wise, gentle man who loved my mother despite her behaviour.

Imagine my surprise when I became aware that men dominated most families. I remember when I lived in England, a friend wanted her sister to invite me to Christmas dinner, but she refused because the ratio of men to women would be uneven. I wasn't raised with that sort of attitude, and I never really thought of men and women being opposite, nor having to be paired.

Even my own children defy traditional stereotypes. My son asked to learn ballet at the age of five, has been a dancer, and is now a choreographer and teacher. My daughter came from a non-sporting family but is mad about sport and has a degree in sports management. I was absolutely fine with this. I allowed my children to do what they wanted. I didn't interfere with their choices.

LACK OF FEMALE ENERGY

I began my career in dentistry at a time when most students were Caucasian males. I was one of the few females in my classes and I recall some people talking about men and women being "opposite". I didn't agree, as I thought we were all people. Once I began studying tarot and astrology, I learned about feminine and masculine energies. In fact, when we see a person's astrology chart, both feminine and masculine energies are contained and we can't tell if the chart represents a man or a woman.

It occurred to me that the problem was in society. There is too much emphasis on masculine energy and not enough on feminine energy in terms of respect and expression. Women in the 1960s had to behave in a masculine way to earn employment and survive in their jobs. There is a movement towards balance today, and things are starting to change in terms of this, for example, collaborative family law—a blend of the feminine and masculine—as opposed to the adversarial approach, which is highly **rational**, **logical**, and **competitive**.

DIFFERENT...NOT OPPOSITE

Women and men are often portrayed as opposite, but I disagree and say they are different. What's wrong with being different? Accepting differences allows us to enjoy the richness and diversity of life, which exists whether we recognise it or not. Unfortunately, because we're in a very masculine-dominated world that thinks hierarchically, people automatically assume that something different has to be better or worse than something else.

There are many advantages in having differences. A differing point of view can stimulate new ideas, help define individuals, and allow us to challenge ourselves or others. When we meet someone who is different, we can ask why we are a particular way and decide if we want to change or remain the same. For example, when I became a vegetarian, people felt very challenged by my decision. One man accused me of expecting others to be vegetarian, but I assured him that wasn't the case and his wife backed me up on this.

Experiencing diversity can create a much more balanced society. We can enjoy different people and cultures. A team with different skills allows us to achieve more and be more effective than if everyone has the same skills. Variety enriches our lives and lifestyles.

Instead of thinking of difference in a **competitive hierarchical** way, we can shift our perception to view it with **flexible awareness** of our **interdependence** and a **holistic** ability to not only **allow** people to be different but rejoice in the richness and diversity it brings.

SOCIAL CONDITIONING

The issue of nature versus nurture in terms of raising children has been debated over and over, but it seems to me that it is nature *and* nurture. These are very complex issues and there continue to be studies conducted on how much girls' and boys' behaviour is innate and how much they are conditioned during their formative years—for example, boys being taught "big boys don't cry" and girls being encouraged to focus on emotions when they play with dolls. Social conditioning also exists in stories, such as Cinderella, Sleeping Beauty, and Snow White, where the man is the problem solver and the woman is helpless. Children's books have changed in recent years, but the older children's stories were very gender stereotypical.

When a boy is young, one of the most important people in his life is his mother. As he becomes an adolescent and is developing into being a man, because our society's attitude is that men and women are opposite, it can lead to him believing that he must do everything opposite to his mother. For example, if the mother is helpful, he will think he has to be difficult. It's an intriguing process, and it happened to me. My son was a lovely young boy. When he turned sixteen, he started behaving badly and I said to him, "Look, you're separating from me and that's okay. It's really what you need to do. However, you can do it nicely or you can be nasty about it. You can still separate and be nice". He apologised and learned from that conversation.

As boys grow into adulthood, some have worked out how to access both their feminine and masculine energies, but many have not. *The Man Box: A Study on Being a Young Man in the US, UK, and Mexico* was released in 2017[2], and it characterised the box that young men find themselves in if they internalise and agree with society's rigid messages on how a man should behave.

These characteristics involve society-initiated *rules* that include:

- Don't act like a woman.
- Don't be too loving.
- Don't be too caring.

---

2 Brian Heilman, Gary Barker, Alexander Harrison, *The Man Box: A Study on Being a Young Man in the US, UK, and Mexico* (Washington, DC and London: Promundo-US and Unilever), 2017.

- Don't ask for help.
- Don't be too committed.
- Always be in control.
- Don't be too nice or kind.
- Don't show weakness.

Boys' behaviour evolves from these perceptions. They are still discouraged from crying if they are in pain—either emotional or physical—so they don't allow their tears to be seen. They are encouraged to be **powerful** and **strong** and not get in touch with their emotions because that's too feminine. They are told to be **protectors** and **show no fear, be in charge, make decisions,** and remain **aggressive** and **tough.** With this, the boys turn into men who exhibit these behaviours towards women. It filters down and is ingrained in everything from religion to corporations. Men also need to be aware that when they denigrate the feminine, *they are actually denigrating an aspect of themselves.* This can turn into an unconscious inner conflict.

I went to an all-girls school where we were expected to go to university if we were able. I studied sciences and experienced social rejection from boys because of that. I attended a dance and was with a boy who was also in his last year of school. We were on the dance floor when he asked me what subjects I was studying in my final year of school. I said, "English physics, chemistry, calculus, applied mathematics, and pure mathematics". He said he needed to get a drink and left me standing on the dance floor! Unfortunately, the attitude in those days was that you were superior if you studied sciences rather than humanities, and he was studying humanities. I don't agree with this. I believe that we all have different skills and none are superior to others.

When I moved on to study dentistry, there were very few girls in the program. During a chemistry class, a male student told me I should be at home learning how to cook, rather than doing chemistry. I responded, "Well, if I can follow a chemistry experiment, I can certainly follow a recipe".

Historically, the division between the genders occurred because of childbirth. Men have a minimal role in the process, whereas women can be significantly incapacitated for a few months before birth, through labour, and then beyond as they recover from childbirth and nurse their baby. This led to men assuming the role of protector. It's not that women were weak or helpless, but they needed men they could trust when they were in this vulnerable state. That symbiosis is the reason why humans survived and why we are here today.

However, the world has changed. In modern society, women have less children and a significant majority of women and their children survive childbirth. The population has moved to cities and no longer needs protection in the same manner. New occupations have arisen, and people live longer. This has been a huge challenge for society and has left men, who were so comfortable in their masculine-dominated world, confused. Men's traditional role of "protecting women and children" has evolved into them being dominating and controlling in all aspects of life. This is now being challenged by women, and for some men that challenge has been distorted into vengeance and an out-of-control masculine behaviour. Other men express their confusion and vulnerability as a result of this change from their traditionally defined role as protector and income-earner by saying that often they don't know what is expected of them anymore.

MOVING TOWARDS BALANCE

Of course, masculine energies are important and necessary, but in our Masculine-Dominated Society (M-DS), when they are not balanced with feminine energies they become distorted, causing the feminine energies to become damaged and underutilised. Finding the balance is crucial, and it is generally easier for women to achieve balance because they grew up in a M-DS and therefore have a greater understanding of both energies, whereas men often find the feminine energy foreign and strange. In this regard, men can be disadvantaged because they are frequently stuck in the stereotype, whether they want to be or not. They may not want to go to war. They may want to be a nurse. It's unfortunate when they are pigeonholed into what society deems as appropriate in the same way that women have been stereotyped into roles of housewife, mother, and female-dominated work.

When men start understanding and utilising their feminine and masculine energies more consciously, they don't have to feel challenged by women. They will feel more comfortable around women because they will understand them better and therefore won't have to put on all those antics to maintain their fantasy of superiority. They can relax and enjoy women for who they are, while still recognising that they're different...not opposite.

If we can understand and accept that women and men are not the polar opposites we're made out to be, we can bring forth our full selves and flourish. We have permission to be who we want to be and do what we want to do. We don't have to be stuck in a claustrophobic stereotype, and we can relate to the other gender in a healthy, respectful way.

Having established that people—regardless of gender—have feminine and masculine energies and therefore women and men are different—not opposites—we can move on to another shift that needs to occur.

CHAPTER 2

Woman Is No Longer Man's Possession

When a baby is born, we know who the mother is but not necessarily the identity of the father. When patrilineal inheritance was first introduced, men began to control women's sexuality, and therefore their lives, in order to know their children were actually theirs. This led to women becoming a possession of men, with the overt and subtle practices and traditions of controlling and dominating women, often by the unspoken threat of violence and/or poverty. Now, with DNA testing, there is no excuse for men controlling women.

I've never viewed myself as a possession, so in 1977 when I married my husband, I refused to be given away by my father and I didn't change my name. Society still continues with these messages and traditions of possession where women are given away and/or take on their husbands' names. In books and movies, especially older romances, the girl has limited choices and often becomes the man's possession. These are all pretty obvious signs of a Masculine-Dominated Society (M-DS).

THE WAGE DISCREPANCY

In theory, women have begun to earn equal pay in the last few decades, but they still aren't paid equally, a concept that is no doubt connected to the idea that women, being property, don't need money.

In 1972, having lived in England for three years, I returned to Melbourne, Australia and was offered a job at a hospital. It was supposed to be a first-year job, but I had graduated five years prior. They were desperate for someone to fill the role, so they offered me fifth-year pay with postgraduate qualifications, which was what I deserved. However, when my paycheque came, it was first-year pay and not what I had been promised.

I mentioned this to my father, who asked if I had a letter of offer from the hospital. I did but hadn't replied to it. He asked me if I really wanted the position. I hadn't been treated well, so I didn't much care. He typed out a letter for me, which I sent to the hospital. I then visited the administrator, who hadn't yet read the letter because they were usually letters of acceptance. After speaking to the administrator, he said he would look into the matter.

After the next paycheque, I still hadn't heard from the administrator. I returned to his office and was told that the board had agreed to offer me third-year pay. By this time, I was happy to leave the job if they didn't do as they had promised. I told him, "You think I don't need the money because I'm a woman, and I don't like that attitude".

He turned bright red and, after further delays, I was finally given the salary promised.

More recently, my daughter and several male counterparts had exactly the same jobs, but she earned $10,000 less per year.

These things happen all the time. Work that is traditionally considered women's work is grossly underpaid. For example, teachers and childcare workers are underpaid professions, even though they take part of the responsibility for the development of the next generation. That's a very important job! Meanwhile, people who have unproductive work playing on computer screens make millions of dollars. It makes very little sense.

A year after I left the hospital, a bank refused to lend me money for a house because I'm a woman. I earned twice as much as my brother at the time and wanted to borrow half as much as him, but I was refused, while he had no trouble getting a loan. Again, my father stepped in to help but, in the end, he had to guarantee me, whereas he didn't have to guarantee my brother. I was lucky, because other women my age were unable to get housing loans and consequently were not able to develop that sort of security for their retirement.

A woman is her own person and not someone else's property. Having moved on from the days when women were not allowed to own property, surely it is now important that all women receive genuine financial opportunities equal to men.

VIOLENCE RESULTING FROM ATTITUDES OF POSSESSION

My ideas of not following the status quo came from being raised to be independent. I obtained a university degree, earned my own living, and paid taxes, so I never saw any reason why I should belong to a man. However, women's issues were really highlighted when I heard that the police wouldn't step in during a reported domestic violence situation. I was appalled because violence is violence, and if two men were fighting, the police would have stepped in. In those days, it was said domestic violence was a family matter and none of their business—in essence saying a man is allowed to hit a woman because she is his possession and he is allowed to control her.

Although work is currently being done on the domestic and family violence front, there are still communities where it's an appalling problem. In Australia, progress was made after a violent situation in February 2014. Eleven-year-old Luke Batty was playing cricket at a sports centre in Melbourne, Australia, when his father, Greg Anderson, approached the field and attacked Luke. Anderson beat and stabbed his son to death before being shot by police at the scene. Anderson was taken to a hospital, where he later died. Luke's mother, Rosie Batty, went on to campaign for improvement in services to assist family violence victims. She was also named Australian of the Year in 2015 for her work. The government took notice and change began.

In this situation, both mother and father were angry. The difference was in how they handled it. The father took his terrible rage out on his son, with obviously *destructive* anger. Most people consider temper tantrums to be the only form of anger, but Luke's mother, Rosie, expressed her anger *constructively* by choosing to work to change the system.

Ninety-five percent of women who are killed are murdered by their partners or husbands. A lot of the men probably don't *mean* to kill their wives, but it appears to be a perception of possession: *do what I say, or I'll get angry.*

As the government took note of Rosie's efforts, we saw a change in some of the messages around domestic violence. Advertisements now show men yelling at their wives, not necessarily physically striking them. This is a positive step as, in the past, it was considered okay to be verbally abusive as long as you weren't physically abusive. In other words, verbal and emotional abuse were not considered to be "domestic violence". Society has come to realise that verbal and emotional abuse can be just as damaging.

It's interesting that a traditional children's nursery rhyme is:

Sticks and stones can break my bones
But words will never hurt me.

When in fact:

Sticks and stones can break my bones
And words can *break my heart and my spirit.*
—Robert Fulghum ("and my spirit" added by the author)

HIERARCHY, ANGER, AND BLAME

Analysing domestic violence according to the masculine principles in the table, a scenario can play out in this way: there is a **linear**, **rational**, **logical**, **analytical** perspective with a **hierarchical** belief that women are the property of men and should obey them and be the person they want them to be. If challenged, the partner/husband **reacts** in a **defensive**, **competitive**, **independent** manner, **acting** with **detachment** and **strength** to **control his life** by taking control of his partner/wife; this being fueled by *destructive* **anger**.

In other words, when men believe they are the master of the household, they carry that forward into believing women have to do as they say and be the person they want them to be.

That's completely unreasonable because a woman is her own person.

Emotions are feminine, and the emotion of anger can be

feminine, but when it becomes distorted and damaged by a line-up of unbalanced masculine energies (described in the pattern of behaviour above) it becomes destructive and evolves into violence.

Blaming women goes back as far as the story of Adam and Eve. Eve plucks the apple from the Tree of Knowledge and offers it to Adam. He could have refused, but he took it, and when things went wrong, *he didn't take responsibility for his decision* but instead blamed her. It's the classic masculine-dominated behaviour of not taking responsibility for one's behaviour and then blaming someone else when things don't work out. Men and women who operate from distorted masculine energies continue to do it today. For example, they come home from a bad day at work and take it out on their spouse.

ANGER IS ONLY A TOOL

Anger is an energy that allows us to accomplish things. As I discussed above, it can be constructive or destructive. If I come home to my house that's in a mess, and I've finally had enough, I'll use the anger to tidy up. That's constructive anger—it is an energy that says, "There's something wrong here. I'm responsible for it and I'll fix it". In this case, the **rational logical action** is tempered not only by **emotion** but also **imagination** and **holistic** thinking. I am **proactive** (combining **reactivity** and **reflection**) and my **detachment** is balanced by **sensitivity, allowing** the ability to behave **sensibly**.

Destructive anger (as described above) is the temper tantrum. Not wanting to clean up, the person demands that someone else does it, or smashes things instead. It's out of control and damaging.

Of course, feminine masculine energy can work in the opposite way, too, where masculine energy is not utilised and the feminine is excessive. An excessive amount of feminine energy might be someone who is incredibly passive and doesn't achieve. The person might be emotional without a practical outlet, wafting along in life.

WOMEN WITH DISTORTED MASCULINE ENERGY

While destructive anger comes from distorted masculine energy, it is not exclusive to men. Sometimes, it's women who exhibit destructive anger. My mother, for example, was dominating and controlling. She wasn't physically abusive, but she could be verbally abusive and unaware of the impact her behaviour had on other people.

She once told me that when I was a baby, she followed the doctor's orders because doctors were viewed as gods in those days. He told her to feed me according to time, not according to hunger. If I cried, she was to put me down at one end of the house, then go to the other, turn the radio on, and ignore my crying.

One day, she came in to find me holding my breath and blue in the face. She rushed to the telephone, phoned the doctor, and he said, "Hit her and she'll start crying again".

That's what she did, when I just needed to be fed.

I believe that had a huge impact on me, in terms of being frightened to ask for what I want. Because babies and young children tend to generalise things, I thought if I asked for what I wanted, I would be hit, literally or metaphorically. Because she was my mother and had many good qualities, too, I put up with her behaviour, as my father did.

MOVING TOWARDS HEALTHY RELATIONSHIPS

Holistic thinking is an important aspect of Feminine Masculine Balance (FMB). It's the capacity to see the big picture and to see other people's points of view without necessarily having to agree with them. We can simply see them as different. Masculine, hierarchal thinking alone doesn't operate that way. It's either/or, divisive thinking.

Seeing the big picture and understanding that it's okay to be different requires **intuition** and **imagination** along with the respect and **sensitivity** to **allow** others to have different perspectives. All of this occurs as a result of blending the feminine with the masculine.

PATTERN OF BEHAVIOUR: FMB RESOLUTION OF A DOMESTIC DISAGREEMENT

In contrast to the Pattern of Behaviour: Domestic Violence, if a man can balance his masculine energies with the feminine intuitive,[f] emotional,[f] imaginative[f] perspective and a holistic[f] belief that his wife/partner is her own person and should be able to make her own decisions, then if there is a disagreement, the partner/ husband can be proactive[b] in responding[b] in a trusting,[b] compassionate,[b] and flexible[b] way to collaborate[b] with his wife/partner in finding a resolution.

Note: The superscripts f—feminine, m—masculine, and b—blend refer to the words in the *Blending Some Feminine and Masculine Principles* table.

Within relationships, it's important to be **reflective** and **collaborative**. Each person needs to be allowed to live their own lives and support one another in a co-creative relationship, exhibiting both the feminine and masculine principles.

In the accompanying table, we look at the differences between healthy intimacy and toxic intimacy, with the goal of moving towards healthy relationships. It is clear that to achieve healthy intimacy, a balance of the feminine and masculine is needed.

TOXIC INTIMACY VERSUS HEALTHY INTIMACY

TOXIC INTIMACY	HEALTHY INTIMACY
Obsession with finding "someone to love"	Development of self as first priority
Need for immediate gratification	Desire for long-term contentment; relationship develops step by step
Pressuring partner for sex or commitment	Freedom of choice
Imbalance of power	Balance and mutuality in the relationship
Power plays for control	Compromise, negotiation of taking turns at leading
No-talk rule, especially if things are not working out	Sharing wants, feelings, and appreciation of what your partner means to you
Manipulation	Directness
Lack of trust	Appropriate trust (that is, knowing that your partner will likely behave according to their fundamental nature)
Attempts to change partner to meet one's needs	Embracing each other's individuality
Relationship is based on delusion and avoidance of the unpleasant	Relationship deals with all aspects of reality
Relationship is always the same	Relationship is always changing
Expectation that one partner will fix and rescue the other	Self-care by both partners
Fusion (being obsessed with each other's problems and feelings)	Loving detachment (healthy concern about partner's well-being and growth, while letting go)

Having looked at the way the imbalance between the feminine and masculine can lead to domestic violence, we shall move on to another level of violence—war—in the next chapter.

DISAGREEMENT IS INEVITABLE   WAR IS NOT

CHAPTER 3

Disagreement Is Inevitable, War Is Not

In this chapter, we see that the masculine imbalance of war is domestic violence on a larger scale.

If I'd been born a young man, I would have been in the ballot to be conscripted to the Vietnam War. I certainly wouldn't have wanted to go, and neither did any of my male friends. We could see the futility of war. For my father's generation, enlisting was depicted as a grand adventure. Off they went, with no clear idea what was going to happen—only to return broken and psychologically damaged. This was then passed on to the next generation as intergenerational trauma.

When my son worked at the Royal Swedish Ballet, I visited

him in Stockholm. Wandering around the city, I came across a sculpture with a fantastic, powerful statement: a simple revolver with the barrel tied into a knot.

Guns are such lethal weapons, and this was a public display with a very clear message about the relationship between guns and violence.

GUN OWNERSHIP AND GUN-RELATED DEATHS

When Australia faced a mass shooting in 1996, Prime Minister John Howard organised a moratorium on guns, along with a buyback scheme so that people could sell their guns back to the government. Although gun regulations vary from state to state and people tend to guard what they have very jealously, he persuaded all states to agree on gun restrictions. Theoretically, only farmers who wanted the ability to shoot feral animals, and people in shooting clubs, were to be left with guns. In 2017, there was another amnesty on guns so that people could turn in any they had that were illegal.

Criminals, of course, will have illegal guns, but overall, these measures have reduced the guns in Australia. According to GunPolicy.org, in 2016 in Australia, the civilian firearm possession was 13.7 guns per 100 inhabitants and 1.04 firearm-related deaths per 100,000 people. In the United States there were 101.5 firearms per 100 inhabitants and 11.92 firearm-related deaths per 100,000.

Clearly, gun-related deaths are associated with the level of gun ownership. Many of the deaths are accidents or crimes of passion, and if the guns aren't accessible, those deaths are less likely to happen.

One of the key differences between Australia and the United States is that Australia does not have a multibillion-dollar armaments industry, which, from a masculine-dominated point of view, reflects violence and greed.

People argue that the gun industry makes money for many people—a good **rational**, **logical** argument—but there's a rather determined denial of the consequences of gun ownership. Looking at the big picture—**holistic thinking**—what about the horrendous costs of violence to individuals and the community on many levels, let alone the cost of the various levels of law enforcement? There is also the additional argument that one needs a gun to defend oneself. This is when rational thinking starts to become a bit irrational, because the argument that we need the ability to defend ourselves with guns falls apart if nobody has them.

How many people benefit from the proceeds of the armaments industry compared with the number of people who suffer from its consequences?

Another interesting thing about guns is that they are also

phallic symbols and considered to be very masculine. According to the *Federal Bureau of Investigation's Supplemental Report 1999-2012*[3], in the United States, 90 percent of murders are committed by men, and 67 percent of those use guns. When women murder, which accounts for 10 percent of homicides, only 39 percent use guns.

FUTILITY OF WAR

People who were conscientious objectors in wartime were labelled cowards. There's no doubt that some people are cowardly and don't stand up for others being bullied or defend someone who is clearly in trouble. Cowardice exists, but conscientious objectors basically just don't want to kill people, and not wanting to kill people isn't a cowardly desire.

To turn it around: why is an act of violence considered courageous and an action directed towards peace considered cowardly? I don't know, but I guess it is the way men set up our Masculine-Dominated Society (M-DS) and, to justify war and violence, called the willingness to fight courageous. This turned into an idea that this is simply the way it is. Stuck in a rut! But why do we need to be so controlling, dominating, invading, and aggressive? Why not leave people alone to live in peace?

---

3   "The weapons men and women most often use to kill", The Washington Post, May 7, 2015,
     https://www.washingtonpost.com/news/wonk/wp/2015/05/07/poison-is-a-womans-weapon/.

Extending boundaries comes from greed (a topic I will discuss in Chapter 7). Often the desire for the resources of another country is masked by other excuses. Most of the general population in all countries want to remain where they live. They don't want fighting, nor the destruction of their homes, villages, or cities. To combat the spread of pernicious ideologies like fascism, Nazism, and terrorism, a non-violent response can be much more effective and less damaging than violent overthrows that replace one dictator with another.

In an article, *The Cost of Victory Makes War Futile*[4], Ian Bickerton, an Honorary Associate Professor in the School of History and Philosophy at the University of New South Wales, Australia, discusses the human costs incurred even when victory is achieved: loss of lives, impaired futures due to severe injuries, mental illness, unemployment, homelessness, domestic violence, divorce, and crime. In addition, these traumas can impact the next generation. He also outlines how wars do not achieve their goals and gives numerous examples of what happened in World War II, concluding that the victors and vanquished have all suffered.

There is also, of course, the massive destruction of land and property.

---

4   "The cost of victory makes war futile", ABC News, April 24, 2011, http://www.abc.net.au/news/2011-04-25/bickerton---the-cost-of-victory-makes-war-futile/166666.

DISTORTED MASCULINE ENERGY

The Masculine-Dominated Society assumes wars are inevitable. They're just a part of life. In Chapter 1, I discussed that, to a greater or lesser extent, boys are socialised by distorted masculine attitudes with beliefs such as: they should have no pain or feelings; they should be powerful and strong, protectors, in charge, decision makers, aggressive, and domineering; they should show no weakness; they should be tough, athletic, and courageous; and women are their property or objects. To act like a "real man", boys are supposed to not be too vulnerable, too loving, or too caring. They mustn't act like a woman, ask for help, or be too committed. They mustn't show emotions or weakness.

These attitudes interfere with boys learning to deal with emotions, and can result in emotional immaturity so commonly seen in masculine-dominated people who haven't learned to handle emotions skilfully. This, in turn, leads to problems in handling life's challenges and making soldiers vulnerable to being indoctrinated into perpetrating acts of violence against the enemy in wartime.

In her book *Unmaking War, Remaking Men*[5], Kathleen Barry describes in disturbing detail how the United States army dehumanises soldiers to do their job because how else could these soldiers do what is expected of them?

---

5   Kathleen Barry, *Unmaking War Remaking Men* (Australia: Spinifex Press, 2010), 27-51.

PATTERN OF BEHAVIOUR: VIOLENCE IN WAR

The pattern of violence in war, no matter whether it is caused by a man or a woman, is a masculine-dominated one, operating from a linear,[m] rational,[m] logical,[m] analytical[m] perspective with a hierarchical[m] belief that their way/ideas are the best or the only way/ideas. Those people fighting in a war react[m] in a defensive,[m] competitive,[m] independent[m] manner, acting[m] with detachment[m] and strength[m] to control their own life[m] by taking control of others, and this is usually fuelled by destructive anger (distorted emotion).

Note: The superscripts f—feminine, m—masculine, and b—blend refer to the words in the *Blending Some Feminine and Masculine Principles* table.

CHANGING THE PATTERN OF VIOLENCE

War and violence are distorted masculine energies. This attitude of war, rape, and aggression is widely seen on TV and in movies. Executives say the reason there is so much war and rape on TV and in movies is because there's a desire to fight and to rape women, and they can get away with it because it is part of a story. These images simply maintain our masculine-dominated culture. Certain members of society are so stuck watching violence and atrocities to the point they are desensitised, or even crave it.

In terms of the *Blending Some Feminine and Masculine Principles* table, this aggressive behaviour is *not* based on compassion *nor* recognising we're **interdependent**. It's *not* based on **collaboration** *nor* being **sensitive** to other people's needs. It's *not* **holistic**. It's all about someone wanting to feel like a ruler; **dominating**, **controlling**, and feeling more superior. Killing in a war situation requires **detachment**, *lack of* **sensitivity**, and lack of **compassion**.

When distorted, the masculine energy of **controlling one's own life** spills over into controlling other people as well. This can lead to dictators desiring to extend the boundaries of their country to control even more. Their reaction is **detached**, **defensive**, **competitive**, and **independent**.

If the attitude that war is inevitable is a masculine-dominated attitude, how can we deal with wars differently? Nelson Mandela, for example, started off with a violent outlook and then changed his mind. We need to shift our thinking towards war being an aberration, not an event that's inevitable. Gene Sharp, author of *From Dictatorship to Democracy*[6], writes about removing cruel and despotic rulers using non-violent means. It's challenging, certainly, but it can be done. Non-violent/peaceful solutions are more effective and less destructive. Violence breeds violence. World War I was designated as the "war to end all wars", yet wars keep happening. The only way to achieve peace is through peaceful means.

6   Gene Sharp, *From Dictatorship to Democracy* (New York: The New Press, 2012).

Civilised, mature, balanced people negotiate their differences. They don't just get into an "us or them" situation and fight it out. As we know, words are powerful, so what if, instead of a Department of Defence, we had a Department of Peaceful Resolution? Believing in a need for defence feeds into the masculine-dominated mentality, prompting a country to defend itself when disagreements arise rather than focusing on ways to resolve conflict peacefully.

To negotiate and use diplomacy, we need to blend the feminine and masculine: the **intuitive** and **emotional** with the **rational** and **logical**. We need to think **holistically**, which requires **imagination** to understand another point of view. Even with someone like Hitler, we need to understand where the despot is coming from in order to undermine him.

We need to **reflect**, negotiate, and recognise that we are **interdependent**, *not* **independent**. We need to be **compassionate** and **flexible**, and **trust** that the situation can work itself out. We need to **allow others to control their own lives** as we are **controlling our own**. All of these blended feminine and masculine attributes are required for negotiation and diplomacy—for peaceful resolution of conflict.

On a fundamental level, after thousands of years, shouldn't we have worked out how to resolve disagreements peacefully? The idea that all wars are fought for the acquisition of wealth is attributed to Socrates. He lived almost two-and-a-half *thousand* years ago. If it was recognised then, and so many people have written about the futility of war since, isn't it time we considered a different approach?

MOVING TOWARDS PEACE

Changing the pattern of violence in war requires opening our minds to embrace feminine energies. We need to make that shift, first of all, to understand that war is not inevitable. Diplomacy can work, and the media could choose to report more diplomatic successes than tragic ends.

PATTERN OF BEHAVIOUR: PEACE

Peace comes from having a holistic[f] approach to any situation. This requires the ability to see another's point of view and, even if one does not agree with it, having the intuition,[f] imagination,[f] and emotional[f] maturity to respect it. This leads to a sensible[b] approach to disagreements, thus recognising that we are all inter-dependent[b] and can be proactive[b] in responding in a compassionate,[b] flexible,[b] trusting,[b] and discerning[b] way to collaborate[b] with others to find integrated[b] solutions.

Note: The superscripts f—feminine, m—masculine, and b—blend refer to the words in the *Blending Some Feminine and Masculine Principles* table.

The media could make the decision to report on power correctly—which we'll discuss in Chapter 11—or report on things other than violence. If they have to be sensational, they can report sensationally about non-violent resolutions and diplomacy.

Change is likely to take time, but small shifts are evident. Many more people are interested in diplomacy rather than war. For example, when the Iraq war occurred, Britain and Australia joined the United States because they were allies, but many European countries simply wanted diplomacy.

As the paradigm shift occurs, we can begin to achieve balance. It may take several generations, but I think change is possible and the tide is turning.

Balancing the feminine and masculine can help eliminate war, but it is also necessary for a more effective approach to the environment, as we shall see in the next chapter.

YOU CAN'T EAT MONEY

CHAPTER 4

You Can't Eat Money

Money alone won't solve the world's problems, especially those concerning the environment.

Madagascar is advertised as a living Eden, and, until recently, it was. I read about the country before a recent visit, and the history is amazing. Home to the dodo bird, Madagascar had a rich biodiversity, flourishing and incredible. Sadly, it's not just the dodo bird that has gone extinct; many species have been lost or are near extinction now. While we were there, we saw the last two remaining wild, bamboo-eating lemurs—a father and daughter who will not reproduce. Once they die, their kind will be gone. Why? Because of the massive and growing human population.

The rapid growth in Madagascar is a huge problem for humans and even worse for the environment. We did see beautiful areas on the trip, but most had been swallowed up in human development. Many of those humans are living in poverty, with an agrarian attitude likely backed by religion, raising their many children to work in the fields. Meanwhile, a small minority of the population remains both wealthy and hidden away from it all.

I went to Madagascar to see wonder and beauty, but instead, it was the first time I thought of "Man" as the predator. There was beauty, yes, but the guides who are trying to preserve what remains face an uphill battle. There's more human intervention and destruction than not, and it's only going to get worse as the population increases.

Bhutan, another place I travelled to recently, faces a similar fate with modernization. It is certainly better managed than most countries. No one is permitted to traverse some of the spiritual mountains. This provides protected areas, and that helps preservation—but the expansion of the population and people moving away from the countryside are still a threat to the environment.

Even at home in Australia, the land is very different than before Europeans arrived. A couple of years ago, I walked in the MacDonnell Ranges in Central Australia before visiting my son and family in Germany. We drove through Switzerland on our way to Corsica. It was quite an experience to see both landscapes in a short space of time.

The Swiss Alps are only 50 million years old, whilst the MacDonnell Ranges in Central Australia are 300 million years old. Not only does Australia have less rainfall than Europe enjoys, but, being so much older, the soil has different minerals and composition. European farming practices are appropriate for a relatively young country, but not so in Australia, and they have caused a great deal of damage. Some people are attempting to restore the land, to a certain extent, and adjust their farming to practices more appropriate to this land.

But the reality is the Earth is changing, and we are changing it through masculine-dominated attitudes of **greed** and **expansion**.

CONSTANT EXPANSION CREATES DESTRUCTION

In terms of the Feminine Masculine Balance (FMB), domination and control of the Earth is masculine without the feminine balance of **holistic thinking**, **sensitivity**, and a recognition of the consequences of our actions. It's treating the Earth as though it's inert instead of a living system. Greed leads to mass production (**quantity**); **straight-line** thinking leads us away from recycling; **detachment** and **hierarchal** thinking leads to insensitivity to other animals and a belief that we are superior to all. It also comes from religion—as we shall see later—and the belief that "man" has dominion over the Earth.

Some people are better at taking care of the Earth than others, though no one has really resisted these patterns of thought completely. Bhutan used to be more restrictive of tourists in their country because they had seen the environmental impact of unrestricted numbers of backpackers in Nepal. But things are changing. Often, the shift has to do with population numbers—the more people there are, the more food, clothing, and shelter they need.

Bhutan was living in what amounts to Medieval times until about the 1950s, when their king decided it was time to join the modern world. The first mock democratic election (to familiarise people with the process) didn't happen until April 2007, and it was followed by their first non-partisan democratic election in December 2007. This modernization was inevitable and, of course, it has its advantages, such as the abolishment of slavery and introduction of modern medicine. However, it's the same story we see over and over again. People become educated, there's an industrial revolution, they want jobs, the country expands, they want bigger houses, and so on. Human expansion tends to set these things into motion.

This all seems overwhelming. I once read a quote that sums up our dilemma quite nicely:

"When the last tree is cut,
When the last river is emptied,

When the last fish is caught,
Only then will man realize that he cannot eat money[7]".

Some people might think it's naïve, but I see that quote as absolutely spot on, coming from a place of vision rather than greed. Whoever wrote it is clearly a balanced individual, with insight and understanding rather than an imbalanced, masculine-dominated approach to the environment. It's important for our future that people who are still imbalanced wake up from their insensitivity to see that there are consequences to their behaviour—to see that the masculine-dominated mentality has become a machine, marching forth and destroying the planet.

DOMINION OVER THE EARTH

Clearly, I'm not religious, but I'm familiar with the passage in Genesis that implies the human animal is more important than other animals:

"And God said, 'Let us make man in our image, after our likeness, and let them have dominion over the fish of the sea and over the fowls of the air, and over all the earth, and over every creeping thing that creepeth upon the earth'". (*King James Bible*, Genesis 1:26)

---

7   I once read this verse in a chain email which was claimed to have been seen on a road sign in Bhutan. Variations of this have been circulating and attributed to a number of people and organizations.

There are other interpretations of this passage, but masculine-dominated people interpret it in just one way. The basis of their idea is that man can dominate and do what he likes because he is in charge. There seems to be the attitude that it doesn't matter if some animal species become extinct because there are plenty more.

There's a lack of understanding of the importance of bio-diversity on the planet and the **interdependence** between all of the animals, plants, and habitats. Rivers need a variety of plants to attract the various creatures that help the ecosystem. Different animals and different plants need different things, and they are all interconnected. Biodiversity is important for many things including a larger number of plant species, resulting in a greater variety of crops for food, medicines, wood products, and breeding stocks. Biodiversity also provides protection of clean water sources and speedier recovery from unpredictable events; it aids in breaking down pollutants, which contributes to climate stability; and it offers environments for recreation and tourism. **Hierarchal thinking** and **detachment** keep us from understanding diversity because masculine-dominated people see one thing as more important than another, in a vertical alignment, rather than understanding the broader concept of **interdependence**. It is the combination of the straight line and circle producing a spiral of abundant evolution.

PEOPLE AND THE ENVIRONMENT

Straight-line thinking tells us to keep going in the same direction without looking around to see the consequences of our actions. We keep going forward like an arrow, taking what we want and developing what we want without being sensitive to the consequences. There is also a mistaken belief that the more money one has, the more superior and "powerful" (really controlling and dominating) one is. As we shall see in Chapter 7, there's more to life than money, and many ordinary people are doing extraordinary things that are vital to our community. These often **sensitive, compassionate, nurturing** people are usually not wealthy in a monetary sense and have no thought of being superior. They are, however, wealthy in other ways.

Combining the **hierarchical** belief that "man has dominion over the Earth" with the belief that "the more money one has the more superior one is" can be analysed in a **rational, logical** way and, from a **hierarchical** perspective, as the best way. These people also often act in a very **independent, competitive, defensive, insensitive,** and **reactive** way.

PATTERN OF BEHAVIOUR: MAN AND THE ENVIRONMENT

A rational,[m] logical,[m] hierarchical[m] belief that "man has dominion over the Earth" and all its creatures is interpreted as domination[m] and control.[m] This, combined with the belief that "the more money I have (quantity[m]) the more superior and powerful (controlling[m] and dominating[m]) I am", can lead to unsustainable use of the planet's resources and creatures, and being detached[m] from the consequences of this sort of behaviour.

A holistic[f] approach involves having the intuition,[f] imagination,[f] sensitivity,[f] and awareness[b] of the consequences of human activities on, and our interdependence[b] with, the environment and its creatures. This allows us to trust,[b] respond,[b] and be proactive[b] in a flexible[b] and mindful[b] way, to sensibly,[b] compassionately,[b] discerningly,[b] and knowingly[b] integrate[b] our activities and needs with those of the planet and its creatures.

Note: The superscripts f—feminine, m—masculine, and b—blend refer to the words in the *Blending Some Feminine and Masculine Principles* table.

Another characteristic of masculine-dominated thought is the either/or thinking, which tells us we have to prioritise *either* the economy *or* the environment, but not both. When we blend the masculine with the feminine, we can develop the **sensible awareness** to have **integrated knowing** that it can be this *and* that—the environment *and* the economy.

Straight-line thinking tends to be resistant to change and wants to ignore that life continues to change. In my lifetime, there have been enormous changes in the job market, and they will continue to change as they always have. For example, the closing of coal mines has people worried. They are being replaced by renewable energy sources such as solar and wind power systems. These industries offer jobs and, as they develop, can employ even more people. Unfortunately, the transfer of employment won't be easy. It never has been. However, to bounce back from adversity we need to be resilient—a blend of the feminine and masculine. Adapting to change requires being able to see a bigger (**holistic**) picture and having the **intuition** and **imagination** to **reflect** on what has happened. Amongst other things, we need to be **flexible**, to **trust** and be **proactive** to move on in our lives. There is going to be a short-term loss for long-term gain. FMB will help us get there, whereas narrow, straight-line thinking leaves us stuck in destructive anger and resistance.

It's time to challenge the status quo. A Masculine-Dominated Society (M-DS) is comfortable the way things are, so it's inclined to just keep going along that straight line. By understanding FMB, we will be able to work out ways of sustaining the environment within a better framework for handling the economy.

MOVING TOWARDS A HEALTHY PLANET

The truth is that we are dependent on the planet and have

a responsibility to care for it. As we come to understand this, we can begin to bridge the gap between human needs and the environment and get decision-makers to see it as well. It's important that they make the paradigm shift to understand that we need to live in FMB rather than in masculine-dominated ways of living, thinking, and operating in the world.

Even if someone lived on a deserted island, without anyone or anything else, they'd still depend on the indigenous plants and animals, and the fish in the sea. We all depend on one another. On the other hand, wealthy people tend to take this interdependence for granted, thinking, "I can afford it, so I'll have it". But what is available for them if someone hasn't made it? What house would they have if someone hadn't built it? What food or clothing would they have without someone growing and harvesting and processing it for them? It's easier to just not think about our **interdependence** and what's involved in producing the items they have bought.

Change is tricky, and though we can see that the tide is turning, there are still people so stuck in their masculine-dominated way of thinking that it might be too difficult for them to change. I'm sort of hoping that they're simply dying out. Some of their progeny will take on those attitudes, while more and more people continue to change, and eventually, in time, we'll arrive at the tipping point.

We have seen how important FMB is for the health of the planet. In the next chapter, we will look at how it plays out in human health.

CHAPTER 5

Most Doctors Are Specialists in Disease, Not Health

It's important that doctors are specialists in disease, but in terms of Feminine Masculine Balance (FMB), health is more than an absence of clinical symptoms.

As I mentioned in Chapter 2, five years after I graduated from dental school, I returned from overseas and was offered a job in a general hospital as an assistant to faciomaxillary surgeons. I also had a part-time position at the Children's Hospital. Because a child's skull is so much bigger in relation to their face, a broken jaw is often fatal, but we did see a few cases. As a children's dentist, I therefore thought it would be a good experience to work in the faciomaxillary unit for a year.

Most of the doctors were men, behaving in their usual masculine-dominated way. All the nurses were female, and they were behaving in an unbalanced way, too. This is when I became aware that, when there is just one gender working together, behaviour can become unbalanced.

During that year, I also became aware of the lack of what I would call basic healthcare—like the food choices. At the time, doctors had very little training in nutrition. I've heard that it's improved a bit over the years, but when I worked there, the food at the hospital could only be described as nutritionally inadequate and unappetising. Most of our patients had their jaws wired together, so the blended food provided was even more disgusting. Some lucky patients had relatives who would bring them homemade blended soups.

Unfortunately, most of the surgeons tended to treat patients like lumps of meat—except the private patients, whom I noticed they'd schmooze up to. They would treat their patients as cases instead of people, often talking in front of them and apparently oblivious to the fact that the patients could hear what they said. The doctors were unaware of the emotional consequences of some of the things they were saying.

WHAT IS HEALTH?

Historically, modern medicine developed from a masculine-dominated **logical, rational, analytical,** and **scientific** approach. This has resulted in extraordinary advances in the understanding of diseases, medicines, and surgical techniques. However, for all those advances, the types of diseases may have changed but the overall incidence of diseases hasn't improved and seems to be worsening. Yes, we are being kept alive for longer (**quantity**—masculine) but with how many diseases debilitating us (**quality** of life)?

In defence of doctors, the logistics are difficult. The number of people requiring treatment is enormous. So, to that degree, the whole process needs to be streamlined. However, what I found was in contrast to my training. As dentists, we try to prevent dental disease. Some dentists are better than others, but at least I did my best to make sure patients knew what was inappropriate to eat, how to clean their teeth properly, and what they could do to focus on prevention rather than cure. These doctors were treating accidents and diseases, and I didn't hear much about preventing them.

It seemed to me that doctors were operating from a paradigm of health being the *absence of clinical symptoms* and treating patients accordingly. Perhaps this is one of the reasons why we have so many chronic diseases in Western society today. The problem is that chronic disease can take years, if not decades, before clinical symptoms appear. Major diseases such as heart disease, cancer, and diabetes are chronic diseases that can go unnoticed until it's too late. I remember hearing that when doctors undertook post-mortem examinations on young soldiers who had been killed in the Vietnam War, they had enough atherosclerosis in their arteries to have a heart attack, but because their young arteries were flexible, they had no symptoms of arterial disease.

Being a perpetual student, I started looking into health alternatives. It seemed to me that a lot of the chronic disease could be prevented, or at least reduced, with proper nourishment, hydration, exercise, sleep, self-help techniques, meditation, and hygiene. I also heard on an Australian Broadcasting Corporation radio programme (*Health Report* with Norman Swan) that the greatest improvement in human health over the years has come from the education of women. Nurses, at the time, were all women—mothers, sisters, and daughters were the people doing the actual caring. Doctors might give the drugs, but women care for the patients. So, it seems that hygiene, nutrition, loving care, and connectedness are important to health—not just technology.

When I was younger, I thought any disease was basically in the body. I then learned about emotional, mental, and spiritual effects on health, and that these factors were just as important. This research and experience, over time, evolved my understanding of **health**—which I define as *balance on the spiritual, emotional, physical, mental, creative, and worldly levels.*

There are many practices which assist healing from the perspective of FMB. For example, diet **nourishes** and **sustains** the body. Exercise is important, but it is **active** (masculine) and needs to be balanced with passive stretching (feminine) for **flexibility** and injury prevention. Meditation and **mindfulness** (a blend of **being** and **doing**) is crucial for stress reduction, a more peaceful mind, better memory, and focus. Spiritual practices enhance a person's **compassion** and ability to experience and **integrate** meaning and purpose in life through connectedness to self, others, the arts, nature, and/or a power greater than self.

MASCULINE-DOMINATED MEDICINE

Having trained as a dentist, I was aware that medicine developed from a **rational, logical, scientific** approach. All of the diseases are categorised in **hierarchal, analytical** ways. Unfortunately, doctors tend to get stuck *fighting* disease, which is a very masculine thing to do. It generally leads to other masculine attributes, such as being **detached, action-orientated**, and **controlling**.

Now, there's no doubt that detachment is necessary. I have worked with sick children in hospitals, and if I had not been sufficiently detached I would have been too distressed and unable to help them. But there needs to be a certain amount of sensitivity, too. Psychological, social, and spiritual support are equally important.

In the past, the goal was about finding one single physical cause of an illness—a masculine straight line that reduces things to one. However, we are complex beings, and diseases, particularly chronic diseases, are caused by multiple factors. The masculine-dominated mind has difficulty broadening to deal with multiple causes because it's easier to focus on a single prevailing symptom. Even something as simple as falling over and breaking a leg is not just a physical break. Why did the patient have the accident? Perhaps there were emotional factors such as distress or maybe the person was just distracted. There can be other factors beyond only the physical, even in the most apparently straightforward cases. And the effect of the injury on their life also needs to be considered.

Our masculine-dominated language fights things. We fight disease, fight terrorism, fight drugs—even though the "war on drugs" has been shown to be unsuccessful compared to the more humanitarian approach taken by Portugal, where drugs are still illegal but the use of them has been decriminalised. If a person is caught with an illicit drug they get a small fine and are probably referred to a treatment programme. The public resources spent on drug control have now been transferred to a public health model for treating hard drug addiction. It might not be a perfect policy, but it is definitely more **balanced**, **compassionate**, and effective than criminalising drugs.

SIDE EFFECTS OF PHARMACEUTICAL DRUGS

So often, pharmaceutical drugs have been overused. There are various reasons for this. At times, the prescriber may be unaware of other medications the patient is already taking, or patients are given drugs when they do not need them. This is especially the case with antibiotics and narcotic painkillers.

There is also a concern regarding the "side effects" of drugs. All drugs have an *effect* on the human body. The "wanted effect" targets the intended symptoms and any other outliers are called "side effects", which makes them sound lesser than the target effect. It's a bit like the term "collateral damage" in war—it certainly sounds better than what it really means: civilians being killed. These side effects of a drug can lead to a patient taking a number of other drugs to counteract them. An example is a patient being prescribed amitriptyline for insomnia. Common "side effects", particularly in the elderly, are constipation, urinary incontinence, dizziness, dry mouth, and dry eyes.

To "treat" these effects, the patient may finish up with five medication therapies for the one condition.

The pharmaceutical industry often has a conflict of interest with doctors and patients. They sometimes over-promote drugs by referencing biased or altered medical studies. They also sometimes encourage sales via aggressive advertising campaigns or offering incentives to private doctors to push the product. This leads to unnecessary use of the drug or unnecessary dosage—which, of course, relates back to masculine-dominated greed.

A BROADER APPROACH

Disease itself is dis- (lack of) ease. It's a lack of balance on all levels of our being: physical, mental, emotional, spiritual, worldly, creative, etc.

For millennia, however, healers have recognised that the mind, body, and spirit are a self-healing organism, constantly striving to maintain internal stability.

Claude Bernard, a French physiologist, first introduced homeostasis in the nineteenth century. Norman Doidge, in his book *The Brain's Way of Healing: Remarkable Discoveries and Recoveries From the Frontiers of Neuroplasticity*, describes Bernard's view as "the ability of living systems to regulate themselves in their inner environment, and to maintain a stable state in the body, despite the many influences, both external and internal, that tend to disrupt that state[8]". It counteracts any influence that would push the system into deviating from the optimum state in which it's evolved to function best. For example, if we cannot maintain a temperature of 37 degrees Celsius (98.6 degrees Fahrenheit), we'll die. If we get too hot or cold, our bodies attempt to return to that temperature. Many of our organs contribute to homeostasis—the kidneys, liver, nervous system, and so forth. So when I say, "allowing the body to heal itself", it is describing homeostasis.

The body can heal itself. Medicine, nutrition, and other therapies assist, but they don't actually do the healing. An analgesic eliminating pain can help us relax, which allows the healing mechanism to function better than if we're very tense and in pain. A cast, in the case of a broken bone, keeps the bone in alignment, which is essential for it to be able to heal correctly but it's the body that actually heals the break. In this way, drugs and interventions are useful and important, but we have to be **discerning** about them and not overuse them. In terms of FMB, **discernment** is a blend of **quality** and **quantity**. We also need to better **trust** (a blend of **allowing** and **controlling**) the body's capacity to heal itself.

---

8   Norman Doidge, *The Brain's Way of Healing. Remarkable Discoveries and Recoveries from the Frontiers of Neuroplasticity* (New York: Viking Penguin Group, 2015), 265.

QUALITY OF LIFE

Balancing longevity (**quantity**—masculine) with **quality** of life (feminine) requires **discernment**. My father died at ninety-eight, and my mother died at ninety-six. People tell me how lucky I am that my parents lived so long, but I can assure you there is no pleasure in seeing someone you love, who has lived a fulfilling and vibrant life, suffering for so long.

My mother had dementia for fifteen years, and there came a time when she had no quality of life. During the final few years of her life she lived in her own little world, locked up in an institution, even though she had told me years before, "Don't let me become a vegetable". I could do nothing about it. We just had to wait for her to die. My father was mentally present but increasingly frail until he couldn't walk. He lived in an assisted facility and had to be lifted by a crane and placed on the toilet. The staff would then go to help other people, leaving my father on the toilet until they had time to return and operate the machine to get him back into bed. He couldn't feed himself properly and didn't like the food they gave him. He gradually wasted away. If you saw a photo of him before he died, you'd think he was in Auschwitz. During the last year of his life, he had to endure what amounted to torture until he died. It was hideous, and I'm still upset about it. Both my parents believed in euthanasia and had joined the Euthanasia Society, but my father couldn't request it because it was illegal.

Life is not just about living longer. It's about the **quality** of life that can be enjoyed. **Discernment** is a blend of **quality** and **quantity**, and when terminal illness, incredible pain, and poor quality of life due to frailty become an issue, doctors and the patient's loved ones should be allowed to **discern** end-of-life decisions. It's what veterinarians do for animals who are suffering.

In a **balanced** society, people would be discerning about euthanasia. They wouldn't just kill people to get rid of them. A friend of mine once raised an objection to me, saying, "If we allowed euthanasia, people would knock off their parents for their inheritance". So, I went home and told my daughter: "If I get dementia, I would rather you euthanise me and get your inheritance than allow greedy investors to steal your inheritance through investing in nursing homes". I believe all nursing homes should be not for profit.

Years ago, I happened to see my parents' neighbour in a park as I walked my dog. He said, "The latest thing to invest in is nursing homes. You can make lots of money keeping people alive". Yet, someone who can't look after themselves, who can't take themselves to the toilet or feed themselves, can't make the choice to die with dignity.

Now, in our state of Victoria, Australia, there has been some limited progress where people with painful terminal illnesses can, with their doctor's judgment, terminate their lives. But, at this stage, they still won't allow it with the elderly, largely because of religious objections.

End-of-life decisions are only a small part of balance and quality of life. When a doctor prescribes a drug, perhaps there is an alternative. If it truly is necessary, perhaps the dosage could be reduced or the effects could be minimized using other health practices. There's no doubt that alternative treatments can require a lot more compliance than just taking a drug. Diet and exercise alone require a good deal of cooperation and understanding from the patient. Ultimately, every individual is responsible for their own health. Doctors can really only offer guidance and then treatment when things go wrong. Unfortunately, some people think that, providing they go to the doctor regularly, they will be okay.

People need to be given choices, but they also need to be educated. Comprehensive health education from an early age is vitally important, but it is seriously undermined by advertisers of highly processed foods, drinks, and other products harmful to health.

Some time ago, I was unable to purchase an imported brand of soy milk. It had been withdrawn from the shops because of high levels of iodine, which can cause thyroid dysfunction. I don't have a problem with that decision, but it would only affect a relatively small section of the population. However, I did wonder what would be left on the supermarket shelves if all products containing sugar (sucrose) were removed. It is well known that, apart from dental decay and obesity, diseases where sugar is implicated—including heart disease, diabetes, cancer, and dementia—have widespread effects on the population. This is one of many examples of how masculine imbalance overrides health concerns. The profit margins of the thriving sugar industry seem to be more important than human health, and manufacturers and investors choose to ignore and/or deny the detrimental effects of their product.

MOVING TOWARDS AN INTEGRATED HEALTH SYSTEM

In 1946, the World Health Organization defined health as "a state of complete physical, mental and social wellbeing and not merely the absence of disease or infirmity". Unfortunately, it seems to be taking a long time for this to be recognised.

PATTERN OF BEHAVIOUR: HEALERS AND CONVENTIONAL WESTERN MEDICINE

Conventional Western medicine is scientifically based, with a rational,[m] logical,[m] analytical,[m] and divisive[m] understanding of diseases, reacting[m] to the symptoms by managing[m]/controlling[m] them with drugs/surgery to prolong (quantity[m]) life. The feminine aspect of healing has a holistic[f] approach focused on the mind/body/spirit, first of all to prevent through adjustments[b] to the body, diet (nourishment[f]) and hydration,[f] rest,[f] meditation[f] and other spiritual practices, exercise,[m] sleep,[f] hygiene,[b] and lifestyle—creativity,[b] music,[b] dance,[b] etc. When a person is unwell, a healer works by supporting the body to heal itself through the practices mentioned above and also other forms of energy and spiritual healing, nutritional[f] supplements, herbal medicines, and/or homeopathics. There is also an understanding and an integration[b] of the knowledge[b] of life cycles[f] and quality[f] of life.

Note: The superscripts f—feminine, m—masculine, and b—blend refer to the words in the *Blending Some Feminine and Masculine Principles* table.

Doctors are called health professionals and are our role models for health. We have "health insurance", which pays us when we are sick, not healthy. Wouldn't this be better stated as sickness insurance benefits? There's nothing wrong with doctors being specialists in disease because we do need to be treated when we are sick. Doctors and the work that they do are very important. But words have power and can be misleading. Do we need to change the way we use the word *health*?

There is a shift towards change, and today there is much more emphasis on healing practices such as diet and nutritional supplementation, but it would be helpful if there were not such a prejudice against alternative ways of treating people. When I was in Bhutan, the traditional healers and the Western healers were in the same hospital. They worked together in harmony rather than seeing each other as the enemy within an either/or framework.

But, even as things begin to change, there are hurdles to overcome.

For example, Dr. Gary Fettke, an orthopedic surgeon in Tasmania, Australia, was concerned about his patients' diets and offered them advice (balancing the masculine therapy with some feminine nourishment). He was reprimanded by the Australian Health Practitioner Regulation Agency, who issued a ban on him giving nutritional advice because they believed he was not qualified.

An Australian Veterinary Surgeon was more successful in incorporating balanced healing. Years ago, when he was a young man, Ian Gawler had cancer. He combined meditation and diet with medical treatment and recovered. In his book, *You Can Conquer Cancer*, he advocates strongly for the power of the mind, meditation, self-help techniques, family and social support, spiritual dimension in life, and the importance of diet for healing cancer.

We are now seeing more and more that alternatives enhance medical treatment. Attaining health is more effective utilising the paradigm of FMB, where healing and medicine are blended and balanced, as in the accompanying table:

MEDICINE	BLENDED	HEALING
Working definition: health is absence of physical symptoms.	Educating the general public how to care for themselves and recognising and utilising any spiritual, mental, emotional, physical, worldly, or creative signs or symptoms of imbalance and working together towards achieving balance.	Definition: health is balance on spiritual, mental, emotional, physical, worldly, and creative levels.
Rational[m] logical[m] suppression of symptoms with drugs, which often produce other symptoms. Keeping people alive without making them well.	Using discernment[b] and trust[b] to utilise appropriate forms of treatment.	Allowing[f] and assisting the natural process by which the spirit/mind/body connection heals itself without recognising the value of medical tests and the value of good medical knowledge.
Focus on fighting[m] disease (controlling[m]).	Integrating[b] the categorising of diseases with supporting[b] the body to heal itself.	Holistic[f] approach to support[b] the body to heal itself.
Main therapy: drugs and surgery,[m] with little focus on diet (nourishment[f]), rest,[f] meditation,[f] exercise,[m] sleep,[f] etc.	Integrating[b] the various forms of healing with discerning use of drugs and surgery.	Focus on supplements, herbal medicines, and/or homeopathics in addition to various forms of energy and spiritual healing, adjustments to the body, diet (nourishment[f]) and hydration, rest,[f] meditation,[f] exercise,[m] diet ,sleep,[f] hygiene, etc. (lifestyle—creativity,[b] music,[b] dance,[b] etc.)
Focus mostly on the body (body mechanics), although this is changing.	Focus on the spirit/mind/body complex.	Focus on the spirit/mind/body complex.
Belief in keeping body alive at all costs (quantity[m] of life).	Using discernment[b] to achieve a balance between quantity and quality of life.	Quality[f] of life and understanding life cycles.[f]
Doctor responsible for health (control[m]).	Trusting[b] the collaboration[b] between the practitioner and client.	Personal responsibility for health.

In the following chapter, we shall see how we need to balance "doing" and "being".

CHAPTER 6

Forget Work/Life Balance, We Need to Balance Doing and Being

In our day-to-day living, the most important balance is not just about work versus play.

Once a friend and I were having lunch. She was feeling stressed because she had a very busy business. She said that she really needed to play more so she could balance it with her work. I thought about it and said, "There's more to it than that. Work and play are important, but they are both activities. What you also need is a balance between activity (masculine) and stillness (feminine). You need to do *and* to be".

In our Masculine-Dominated Society (M-DS), we are rewarded for what we do, not for who we are and certainly not for just "doing nothing". In fact, it's almost a "no-no" to do nothing. My mother was constantly expecting me to do, do, do. When I was older, I would go into my bedroom and pretend to study so that I could have time and space for myself and have the solitude that is particularly important for an introvert like me.

PATTERN OF BEHAVIOUR: WORK/LIFE BALANCE

The "doing"[m] of Work/Life Balance comes from a rational,[m] logical,[m] hierarchical[m] belief that "the more (quantity[m]) I do[m]/achieve, the more superior/better and in control[m] I am". Doing is only one side of the coin. The other side allows for just being[f]—stillness,[f] rest,[f] meditation,[f] and allowing[f] things to be as they are, and for the body to regenerate and integrate.[b] Blending the "being"[f] and "doing"[m] allows[f] us to develop greater sensibility,[b] awareness,[b] knowing,[b] compassion,[b] responsiveness,[b] compassion,[b] discernment,[b] and trust.[b] Laziness ("over-being"), however, is something else entirely, a very passive,[f] weak,[f] and dependent[f] viewpoint that others should "do" for us.

Note: The superscripts f—feminine, m—masculine, and b—blend refer to the words in the *Blending Some Feminine and Masculine Principles* table.

Doing too much is a disease, in the sense of dis-ease or lack of ease. People ask, "What do you do?" not, "Who are you?"

We are called "human beings", but more often, we are "human doings".

VALUING "BEING"

A more balanced approach to life starts with getting enough sleep. Studies show how important it is to get eight hours of sleep (one-third of the twenty-four hours) because while sleeping, the brain shuffles memories and sorts out our life to prepare for the next day by forming new pathways to help us learn and remember information.

During sleep, the body works to repair itself. In this way, it protects our mental and physical health and improves quality of life. In children, sleep also assists with growth and development. Deep sleep triggers the body to release a hormone that promotes normal growth and development in children and teens. This hormone also boosts muscle mass and helps repair cells and tissues in children, teens, and adults. Sleep also plays a role in puberty and fertility. Because sleep helps us pay attention and make decisions, it is important in regard to safety. When I was working in the faciomaxillary unit, we treated many cases resulting from car collisions. I noticed that most serious car collisions were the result of either the driver falling asleep or being intoxicated.

Ongoing sleep deficiency alters activities in some parts

of the brain and leads to difficulties with controlling our emotions and coping with change. It is also linked to risk-taking behaviour, depression, and suicide. Because the body repairs itself during sleep, a deficiency in sleep can result in an increased risk of chronic diseases such as heart disease, blood pressure, stroke, and kidney disease. Sleep also affects the body's response to insulin, resulting in increased levels of blood sugar and therefore an increased risk of diabetes. Because our immune system relies on sleep to stay healthy, ongoing sleep deprivation can even lead to an increase in common infections.

Meditation and relaxation are also important: taking a moment to stop and be totally focused on the body and surroundings. Taking regular moments during the day to de-stress can prevent dis-ease. As we keep practising, we become more mindful of what's happening all the time, and we can focus more on being present and less on being scattered all over the place. "Being" also means taking time for ourselves, getting in touch with our inner resources, feeling good in our own skin, being able to relax, enjoy, and appreciate life, as opposed to connecting our value exclusively to accomplishments and possessions. This requires allowing things to be as they are instead of being concerned about possibilities or a lack of control. In other words, accepting things as they are and being relaxed. It is a challenge to accept the chaos of life and the messy world we live in.

VALUING ACTION—"DOING"

Obviously, we need to be active to care for ourselves and others, earn money, look after our homes, and play. "Doing" is also involved in having an important life mission, providing value, and developing our talents. We are here to enjoy life and we are here to create. "Doing" also gives us a feeling of control and therefore a sense of safety. However, "doing" is not being busy. It means working well and working sensibly. We need to recognise the time necessary for rest and recharge.

Many people in our busy society don't have enough actual physical exercise to keep their bodies functioning efficiently and well. They have sedentary lives even though they are doing so much mental work. Active physical exercise is necessary for health.

I've noticed when people are at the gym or exercising in other ways, they pay little attention to stretching, which is passive (feminine) and vitally important to maintain flexibility. Stretching also helps reduce the risk of injury. In addition we need to recognise that recovery (being) is just as important as exercise (doing). Again, it's a matter of balance.

Technology creates other needs for doing. It is supposed to make life easier, but it doesn't always work that way. Technology creates more communication, as people feel the need to be in constant contact with one another. Before the internet and technology, before the telephone, we had to actually visit someone to see them.

When my grandmother, a farmer, had young children, it was common to offer girls in their late teens board and lodging in exchange for helping in the house. The idea was that they were training to be housewives and mothers themselves. My grandmother used to say that she felt very sorry for the modern mother because "a dishwasher can't hold the baby". Now, I'm not saying that we should go back to her time, but I will say that technology isn't always helpful, nor does it necessarily minimize our work. Once we start buying gadgets, we need more money to pay for them, and they don't have any initiative nor provide the connections that humans can. Robots and such don't have the ability to listen and are not good company. It's a very masculine development—**rational**, **logical**, and **detached**.

Small children play, from the time they wake in the morning until the time they go to sleep at night. It is vital for developing a healthy brain, imagination, dexterity, and physical, cognitive, and emotional strength. They engage, explore, and interact with the world around them through play. Somewhere along our life path, many of us give it up. We become serious, and everything we do has to have a purpose, whereas play is something we do for the fun of it. In their book, *Play: How it Shapes the Brain,*

Opens the Imagination, and Invigorates the Soul, Dr. Stuart Brown and Christopher Vaughan show that purposeless all-consuming play is a biological drive as integral to our health as sleep or nutrition[9]. Our ability to play throughout life is the single most important factor in determining our success and happiness. It is hardwired into our brains and is the mechanism by which we become resilient, smart, and adaptable people. Play is essential to our social skills, adaptability, intelligence, creativity, and ability to problem solve. Yes, we have to work, be responsible, and be productive, but we also need to stop and play.

MOVING TOWARDS BALANCING BEING AND DOING

Most of us suffer from stress. Physical, mental, emotional, and spiritual stress can block healing. When we overdo, we get stressed. Stillness, meditation, relaxation, rest, and sleep allow healing. We need an interplay between doing and being, not one or the other. It is recycling energy. We put out during our active phase and renew during our passive phase.

Consider the following:

---

9   Stuart L Brown, *Play: How it Shapes the Brain, Opens the Imagination and Invigorates the Soul* (New York: Avery, 2009).

Physical stress Mental stress Emotional stress Spiritual stress	Interferes with/blocks	The healing process
Stillness Relaxation Meditation Rest/Sleep	Allows	The healing process

All traditions have practices of prayer, contemplation, meditation, and/or mindfulness as a means to achieve stillness and its many benefits. Currently, most secular mindfulness programmes in the Western world have their roots in Buddhism, Hinduism, and yoga. Some of those who influenced bringing mindfulness to the West are Thich Nat Hanh, Jon Kabat-Zinn, Jack Kornfield, Sharon Salzberg, and Joseph Goldstein.

Mindfulness is maintaining a moment-by-moment awareness of thoughts, feelings, body sensations, and the surrounding environment. It also involves acceptance and the ability to pay attention to our thoughts and feelings without judging them. When we practise mindfulness, our thoughts tune in to what we are sensing in the present moment rather than rehashing the past or imagining the future. When we are very busy, we lose our sense of being in the world and our sense of presence. Mindfulness teaches us to be in tune with the present.

Undertaking a creative activity is a beautiful way of being in the present. I used to teach Art Classes for Inner Peace, with a focus on creativity. In those classes, we would start with a guided meditation to bring us into the space, then we would focus on an element for that session. For Earth, we worked with clay; for water we used watercolours; for fire, wax; for air, pastels; and for spirit, a selection of them all. I encouraged the participants to focus and value the *process* rather than the finished product.

Some people say they aren't creative, when what they really mean is they're not artistic. We are all creative because we create our own lives. Tinkering on cars, gardening, cooking—any kind of creative hobby can provide that space where we're totally in the present rather than being caught up with our busy brain, rehashing the past or imagining the future.

One thing that drives us to do too much is a desire to earn money; money is important in our society but, as we shall see in the next chapter, there is a difference between money and abundance.

CHAPTER 7

Abundance Is More Than Money

From the perspective of Feminine Masculine Balance (FMB), life is more than the accumulation of money.

Yet there are people whose worlds still revolve around chasing money. Even when they succeed in gaining it, they just want more. They are not particularly interested in other aspects of life, they feel empty, and they feel they never have enough, perhaps due to what they didn't get when they were young. They become caught up in a masculine-dominated competitive mindset such as the corporate ladder—a desire to get to the top where money and "success" lie, while fending off everyone else along the way.

I grew up with a wealthy grandfather. He was just good at making money. He and his brother had set up a large poultry farm, which was very successful, and because he was generous, he recycled money instead of just accumulating it. Of course, that is the balance of feminine and masculine, whereas hoarding is straight-line thinking and masculine.

In spite of his wealth, he wasn't very pretentious. He wore ordinary clothes, lived in an ordinary house, and though he owned a Daimler for a little while—with the window between the front and back seat—he decided it wasn't worth having. This was probably because he was a distracted driver and constantly dented his car. It was literally not worth having anything but an ordinary car. That didn't bother him.

His brother, on the other hand, was quite pretentious. My brother and I didn't see that side of the family much because they didn't live in Melbourne. When we were young, we visited their home once, explored it, and called it, "The house that never ends". It just seemed to go on forever! In December 1939, my mother was a bridesmaid at her cousin's wedding, which took place in an aeroplane. The bridal party had the ceremony in the air then landed for the wedding breakfast. It was a big deal in the newspapers and was the sort of extravagant thing their family would do.

My grandfather kept a scrapbook filled with the nonsense the journalists wrote about him because he thought it entertaining. Once, they said he drove a pink Rolls-Royce. That planted the seed in my mind, which has been verified since, that everything I've known about that has been written in newspapers has been incorrectly reported, exaggerated, sensationalised, or is just plain inaccurate.

The broader lesson, however, is that there's a difference between abundance and wealth.

THE SPIRAL OF BALANCE

Masculine energy moves in a linear, straight line that can be symbolic of an arrow, while the feminine is a circle. Life moves in these cycles—day and night, days of the week, seasonal circles, and so on. When we strive to earn vast sums of money only, it's like running on a treadmill, constantly tiring and boring and yet difficult to escape as we keep trying to acquire more.

The traditional treadmill was used to drive machinery and consisted of a large wheel turned by the weight of people or animals treading on steps fitted into its inner surface. They walked in a circle. The modern treadmill is an exercise machine, consisting of a continuous moving belt on which to walk or run. This belt is a squashed circle (distorted feminine) where someone runs or walks in a straight line, all while getting nowhere. Money is only the material aspect of life and by focusing on this singular aspect of life, we are "getting nowhere" in terms of having a life full of richness and diversity. We are limiting ourselves and our happiness greatly.

When balanced, we take the movement of the straight line and the cyclical nature of the circle to create a spiral, which has breadth, width, and depth to its motion. It's important to earn money ethically, acquire a certain amount of savings, and then recycle the rest to enjoy other aspects of life while being aware of our interdependence with the environment and the people around us. This allows for abundance and a breadth and movement to that circular nature that broadens out into a spiral.

THE FEMININE MASCULINE BALANCE OF ABUNDANCE

Abundance is an FMB concept because we need an integration of both energies. Abundance applies to all areas of life—spiritual, mental, emotional, physical, worldly, creative, etc. On the other hand, having only the narrow, straight-line focus on earning and accumulating money often leads a person away from appreciating the many small and apparently insignificant things that make up the richness and diversity of life. A focus on money comes from a greed-pattern belief that the more money I have, the more superior I am, which can lead to being **competitive, detached, controlling**, and **dominating**, often referred to as "powerful". However, it is not true power. It is an addiction, as we shall see in Chapter 11.

PATTERN OF BEHAVIOUR: ACCUMULATION OF WEALTH

There is a rational,[m] logical,[m] hierarchical[m] belief (and straight-line[m] thinking) that "the more money I have (quantity[m]) the more superior and powerful (controlling[m] and dominating[m]) I am". This can come from a feeling of emptiness and lack of self-worth that leads to an excessive desire to possess wealth and/or goods with the intention of keeping them for oneself (rather than recycling[b] them). On their path to achieve wealth, the greedy person reacts[m] by being detached[m] from taking advantage of other people and the effects of their actions on the environment. This path often incudes the masculine aspects of mass production (quantity[m]), and acting[m] in a competitive,[m] defensive,[m] controlling,[m] often independent[m] manner.

Note: The superscripts f—feminine, m—masculine, and b—blend refer to the words in the *Blending Some Feminine and Masculine Principles* table.

Studies have shown that we do need a certain amount of money for food, clothing, shelter, and enjoying our lives, but beyond that people aren't happier. To be happy, we can benefit from things such as abundance of vitality, abundance of well-being, abundance of clarity, abundance of conversation, and abundance of intelligence.

Sharing material, intellectual, emotional, and spiritual resources can lead to a community abundant in all areas of life. Abundance blends **quality** and **quantity** into **discernment**. It's not about squandering money but rather combining good money management and caring for the environment and its people with **common sense**, **awareness**, **flexibility**, and **compassion**.

AN ECONOMIC BELL CURVE

Some people, like my grandfather, are very good at making money. Another is Chuck Feeney, who was the cofounder of the Duty Free Shoppers Group (DFS), which pioneered the concept of duty-free shopping. He lives frugally in a rented apartment, and until he was seventy-five flew economy class, carrying his papers in a plastic bag. He has been described as modest, strategic, compassionate, charismatic, and complex, and I guess that behaviour confuses many masculine-dominated people. Feeney created The Atlantic Philanthropies and, in 1984, secretly transferred his entire stake of DFS to the foundation. His business partners didn't even know he no longer personally owned his share of DFS (over one-third and equal to approximately $500 million).

The Atlantic Philanthropies gave away money in secret for years, all the while requiring that recipients not reveal the source of their donations. In February 2011, Chuck

Feeney became a signatory to The Giving Pledge. He wrote a letter to founders Bill Gates and Warren Buffett, saying, "I cannot think of a more personally rewarding and appropriate use of wealth than to give while one is living—to personally devote oneself to meaningful efforts to improve the human condition. More importantly, today's needs are so great and varied that intelligent philanthropic support and positive interventions can have greater value and impact today than if they are delayed when the needs are greater[10]", leading to the catchphrase "Giving While Living".

Interpreting Chuck Feeney's sentiments in terms of FMB, it is obvious he has a **holistic** approach to the human condition and has **responded** to that. **Responsiveness** is the blend of the feminine **receiving** the proceeds of his business and the masculine of **giving** a portion of it away. He has been **discerning** in the masculine **quantity** he personally needs and has a desire to improve the feminine **quality** of the lives of many people. He has also been **mindfully proactive** with **sensible awareness** and has shown great **compassion.**

Over the course of his life, he has given away more than $8 billion.

---

10 "Atlantic's Founding Chairman Chuck Feeney Joins the Giving Pledge", The Atlantic Philanthropies, February 22, 2011, https://www.atlanticphilanthropies.org/news/ atlantics-founding-chairman-chuck-feeney-joins-giving-pledge.

There are others who have become wealthy due to greed, pricing their products higher and higher so that they can continue to make more money. A clever social economist could probably work out the negative impact on society that comes from making products more expensive than they could be, such as the computer, on which we are all dependent.

There's a bell curve to earnings and how it relates to society. Everyone who has enough money for food, clothing, and shelter is in the middle of the curve. On one end, there is extreme poverty, and on the other end, there's excessive wealth. On 15 January 2017, Larry Elliott, economics editor for *The Guardian*, wrote an article discussing a report from Oxfam stating that, around the world, the eight wealthiest people have the same wealth as the poorest 50 percent[11]. The difference between extremely rich and extremely poor is hard to justify. In a balanced society, there would not only be more wonderful people like Chuck Feeney assisting to reduce the inequities at each end of the bell curve, but society as a whole would also find ways to influence corrupt people to reduce these vast discrepancies.

---

11   "World's eight richest people have same wealth as poorest 50%". The Guardian, January 15, 2017, https://www.theguardian.com/global-development/2017/jan/16/worlds-eight-richest-people-have-same-wealth-as-poorest-50.

MOVING TOWARDS JOYFUL ABUNDANCE

It's not just what we earn, it's what we do with the money once we've earned it. We obviously have to save for old age and retirement. But neither greed and hoarding, nor their opposite as a spendthrift, is balanced behaviour. Money needs to be recycled and spent with **discernment** and good money management. Someone who is balanced will earn money, save a certain amount, then recycle the rest.

PATTERN OF BEHAVIOUR: ABUNDANCE

An abundant person is one who has not only the rational,[m] logical,[m] and analytical[m] ability to manage[m] money but also the intuition[f] and imagination[f] to holistically reflect[f] on the world the consequences of their behaviour and our interdependence.[b] They respond[b] knowingly[b] by being proactive[b] in compassionately[b] nurturing[b] those in need and the planet with common sense,[b] awareness,[b] flexibility,[b] and discernment.[b]

Note: The superscripts f—feminine, m—masculine, and b—blend refer to the words in the *Blending Some Feminine and Masculine Principles* table.

There is a religious concept of giving being more important than receiving. This is interesting because **giving** is masculine and **receiving** is feminine. This is a masculine **hierarchical** attempt to diminish the feminine. How can we **give** without **receiving**? Someone has to **receive**, and, in a sense, they are doing the other person a favour by being willing to **receive**. Some people turn this into a domination and control issue, believing, "I am more important than you because I'm **giving** to you". This can cause the receiver to feel disempowered, uncomfortable, and ultimately reluctant to **receive**.

Another joyful expression of abundance is the concept of "paying it forward". This is when the recipient of a charitable act repays the debt to another person rather than back to the original benefactor. Some people question this because they claim the need for reciprocity, but if we look at the bigger picture, we see that in some circumstances, giving forward can be more beneficial than giving back, and the original benefactor receives the joy of seeing the generosity moving on. The spiral of generosity moves on, and all people benefit from it through their connections. Generosity has been found to make people happier, and happiness has been shown in many studies to render people healthier, more creative and productive at work, and more successful in their friendships and relationships.

This ties into a bigger picture. We often judge the world and other countries on their economy and wealth. Instead of measuring a country's progress in a financial way, what about measuring it in terms of abundance? How much well-being is there? How much contentment, health, and connection is there between citizens? Is there an absence of poverty, addiction, violence, and crime?

Abundance is a more holistic concept because it is applied to all areas of life: spiritual, physical, mental, emotional, worldly, creative, and social. We can thrive when we have abundance in these life areas. We are then truly "wealthy" and happy.

We now move on to the basis of FMB that is balanced parenting.

CHAPTER 8

Parenting Is Priceless

In terms of Feminine Masculine Balance (FMB), children need both parents actively involved with their parenting on a daily basis.

In a Masculine-Dominated Society (M-DS), parenting is considered women's work and, therefore, undervalued. If parenting would finally be recognised as the important profession that it is, this could resolve or prevent many of our emotional, mental, and social problems.

The M-DS defines work as something for which we are paid. We go to work, we get paid. Therefore, the rational, logical argument is that if we are not being paid, we are not working. If we're not working, we're lazy and we're of no value.

When a couple gets together, there are two jobs: breadwinning, or having a job, and "home duties" that involve cooking, cleaning, shopping, gardening, etc. All of this unpaid work is taken for granted. It's undervalued simply because we cannot say, "I get x-thousand dollars per year for doing these things". If we have children, a *third* job is added. It's unpaid, again, so the M-DS lumps it in with all the other home-caring work.

However, parenting is a third job because, after all, being a nanny is not the same as being a housekeeper. They are two different jobs. As I read once, "Having a job is important. Parenting is priceless". It's an interesting observation that resonated with me.

The word *priceless* has meanings that are generally similar in all dictionaries. One of the meanings from the Oxford Dictionary is, "so precious that its value cannot be determined". That is certainly true with parenting. The Cambridge Dictionary also gives the meaning "used to describe a skill or quality that has a high value because it is very useful". Yes, that applies to parenting, too. A third meaning is that priceless is "very amusing", which really is the case so often with children—watching them play is so entertaining. If we consider the word *price* and add the suffix –less (meaning "without"), this definitely relates to the first meaning: "so precious that its value cannot be determined" but it could also relate to "no pay" and I think that's relevant, too.

UNPAID WORK

After working as a dentist for thirteen years, I was satisfied with my career. I chose to take time off to have children and care for them through their toddlerhood, with the intention of returning to dentistry then. Unfortunately, my husband travelled a lot on business. He was invariably away when there were crises, which included the cot death of our first baby, and I was left to do the parenting on my own.

It was then that I worked out that caring for the children—parenting—and caring for the home were two different jobs, and I decided that two jobs are enough for one person, so I didn't return to the workplace. Women, in particular, run into this problem over and over again when they have children: trying to juggle a paid job with parenting. How do you do it all and what to delegate? Even a full-time mother delegates, for example, sending the children to school. Parenting simply requires more than one person. As the proverb says, "It takes a village to raise a child".

Years ago, I was amused to see, in a magazine, an attempt to put a value on parenting and home duties. They calculated rates for chauffeuring, counselling, cooking, shopping, and all the other tasks involved for parenting and caring for the home. With those hours and the comparable professional rates, it worked out that if I were paid for everything I did, I would have been paid more than my husband with his highly paid engineering job.

UNDERVALUED AND UNDERAPPRECIATED

When I chose not to go back to my profession, I was happy being a mother and happy with my decision. But I noticed that I was undervalued and underappreciated by many men and women.

Once, I took a birthday cake to my daughter's school. As I cut the cake, the teacher said scathingly, "Oh, you're so good at cutting up that cake". I quickly responded, "Surgeon's hands". After assuming I had been a dental nurse, that sorted her out.

Things have changed, and these days a lot more men are willing to assist in the home, so it should be easier for women to go back to employment. However, there is still the mental load described as permanent, exhausting, and invisible by a French cartoonist, Emma, in her cartoon, "You should've asked[12]".

The mental load includes the mental work, organising, list-making, and planning that is done to manage one's own life and that of the family. In other words, it is a management job in itself. In the workplace, a project manager is a separate job from a project participant. Most of us carry a mental load about our work, household responsibilities, financial obligations, and personal life;

---

12 "You should've asked", Emma, May 20, 2017, https://english.emmaclit.com/2017/05/20/you-shouldve-asked/.

but what makes up that burden and how it's distributed within households is rarely equal and is mostly carried out by women. This is not only an onerous task for women but can lead to men thinking there is an invisible hierarchy where they feel they are an employee in conflict with the boss. Instead of being unaware of its existence, men can relieve their partner's stress and feel less like an underling by sharing duties *and* the mental load by applying their excellent masculine skills of **rational, logical, analytical management** coupled with the blended feminine/masculine skills of responding with **awareness, common sense, flexibility, interdependence,** and **collaboration.**

For example, if a man has trouble remembering to do a task at the appropriate time, he can use his phone to set a calendar alarm. He can also digitally store the shopping list. It can be helpful to hold a weekly meeting to discuss the upcoming week, swap responsibilities, and even help teach some of the skills one excels at, so the workload is more even. Men could also make sure the children do their chores and consider what could be outsourced—within budget—when it comes to tasks.

Companies now offer flexibility with their positions, making it easier for women who take time off to return when ready, if that's what they want to do. Some workplaces allow men to take paternity leave and offer more work flexibility when the children are young, to allow the mother to be more involved in her own career.

BALANCED PARENTING

After years of experience, I worked out my definition of parenting as "assisting one's offspring to achieve their full potential on all levels of their being—spiritual, mental, emotional physical, worldly, creative, etc".

Children are amazing little beings full of life, energy, and potential, and they deserve all the love and help they can get to achieve whatever they want to do. As we have seen from the introduction, it doesn't matter whether they are girls or boys, they have both feminine and masculine energies, which need to be developed, and this requires input from both parents.

For example, one of the general differences between mothering and fathering is when a child is injured and runs to their parents wanting a kiss and to be all better. The dad is often stuck doing the man box stuff, telling them to suck it up. The mum often has the Band-Aid, a kiss, and lots of comfort. We need a balance between the two responses. Sucking it up is saying you're not allowed to express your emotions, feelings, or being hurt. The opposite extreme is making a huge fuss, out of proportion to the injury sustained. I would tell my children, "Your body's very clever. It will heal itself". I wouldn't have a Band-Aid for everything; I'd say, "Look, your body will develop a little scab to protect the cut and under the scab it will heal itself".

PATTERN OF BEHAVIOUR: PARENTING

Parenting requires not only a linear,[m] rational,[m] analytical[m] approach but also the holistic[f] sensible[f] awareness[f] that the work we put in now will have beneficial results later, especially in terms of child development. Babies are completely dependent[f] on their parents but, as they grow into children and start developing independence,[m] parents need compassion,[b] mindfulness,[b] and emotional[f] maturity to allow[f] this growth. Parents also need intuition[f] and sensitivity[f] to understand the baby's/child's needs; to know[b] how to join a child's imaginative[f] world; responsiveness[b] to deal with them; and trust,[b] discernment,[b] and flexibility[b] to nurture[b] them towards controlling their own lives[f] while allowing others to control theirs[m] and collaborating[b] with them to learn how to navigate life and understand interdependence.[b]

Note: The superscripts f—feminine, m—masculine, and b—blend refer to the words in the *Blending Some Feminine and Masculine Principles* table.

UNBALANCED PERCEPTIONS

There also continues to be a tension between working mothers who think they are more important than women who choose to do full-time parenting. A neighbour once told me that she could tell which women didn't work at a paid job because, in social situations with men, they had nothing to talk about. I think it's sad that talking about assisting the future generation to reach their full potential is not considered important enough for an in-depth discussion.

A study done years ago may still be relevant today—it said that in mixed company, if a woman talks 50 percent of the time she's considered a blabbermouth, and 90 percent of the time people discuss what men are interested in.

I recall sitting around a dining room table at a dinner party where everyone was talking about what the men were interested in. When there was a bit of a break, the women went into the kitchen and began talking about their children. I challenged them: "Why don't you talk about that at the dinner table?"

Men are probably more willing to be involved in and talk about parenting than they were in those days. I used to help as a volunteer at my daughter's school tuckshop (school canteen) and, once a year, to celebrate Father's Day, some fathers would come to work there. The man-ageress said that it was very funny because the fathers would arrive and compare careers—act competitively and jostle for top position in terms of who had the most important job. They would then go on to talk about other topics of interest, but rarely about their children. On the other hand, when the mothers were there, they would talk about their children and any issues that were happening at the school.

WELCOME CHANGES TO PARENTING

During World War II, women took on men's jobs while they were fighting, but as soon as the men returned, women were expected to give up their jobs, many of them unwillingly. Then, in the 1960s, women were forced to show their masculine side in order to receive paid employment in a masculine world. Gradually, women have been able to introduce more feminine energy in the workplace. As a result of women expressing their masculine energies, some men realised that they would enjoy being involved in caring for their children. This is a great step forward. For balance, it is important for children to be brought up by both parents where possible because, as we saw in Chapter 1, men and women are different. In the case of single-parent and same-sex-parented families, they often find a friend or relation of the other gender to provide experiences for the child.

PARENTING AS A PROFESSION

Despite many improvements in social attitudes, one outdated attitude persists. Parenting is not considered a profession or a proper job. It is interesting how this word *profession* has been evolved by the hierarchical M-DS. The

Oxford Dictionary states that the origin of the word *profession* is from "Middle English (denoting the vow made on entering a religious order): via Old French from Latin professio(n-), from profiteri 'declare publicly' Profession derives from the notion of an occupation that one 'professes' to be skilled in[13]". These days, it is generally defined as "a paid occupation, especially one that involves prolonged training and a formal qualification", thus excluding a lot of very skilled workers including full-time parents.

To recognise parenting as an important and skilled profession, of course, challenges the hierarchical M-DS that defines a profession by how much we're paid and how much education and training we have attained.

One time my husband was really fed up at work—he was a workaholic and needed time off. He decided I could go out and "do all the work" and he would stay home with the kids. I told him that there was no job vacancy and, even if there were, he didn't qualify. He assumed that he could just move in and do what I did without any training. Sure, there are no university degrees for parenting, but to assist one's children to achieve their full potential on all levels of their being—physical, mental, emotional, spiritual, worldly, and creative—requires an enormous amount of understanding, and it takes time to learn and develop

---

13   "Profession", Oxford Living Dictionaries, accessed May 31, 2018, https://en.oxforddictionaries.
      com/definition/profession.

the experience. I suggest to anyone who has children that whenever we fill in forms that require us to state our occupation, we include "father" or "mother".

A woman I knew went into business after having brought up five children. She said, "I don't understand why men make such a fuss about business. It's so much easier than bringing up children!"

MOVING TOWARDS BALANCED PARENTING

The imbalance in parenting roles hurts men, too, not only as parents—plenty of men in my generation regret not spending more time with their children—but as children, too. The son looks to the father as a role model, and if the father is only in paid employment, the son is more likely to follow suit. He's also not getting the attention he needs from his father, and the father isn't sharing his affection, time, and life experience with his son, and everything is likely to continue to be imbalanced. A good masculine role model is also important for daughters because they are influenced by how their father treats not only them but also the women around them. Daughters seek their father's approval and, if this is encouraging, supportive, and reassuring, it can lead to good self-esteem and self-worth. It also helps them learn how to relate to men.

The truth is that men can find the time if they make the

effort, and they could find even more time if the corporate world started recognising the importance of parenting and allowing everyone to have flexible working hours.

I once heard a lovely story from a man who realised he needed to be more involved with his children. When he came home from his job, he played in the street with the children. Soon, the neighbours' children joined in and, if he wasn't there after school, they would ask his wife where "Mr. Smith" was. Clearly, they enjoyed spending time with a masculine figure. "Mr. Smith" said that he didn't regret it one little bit. He spent every evening with his children, which made his relationship with them so much stronger, and he believes they are now better adults as a result of it.

Some men say that they would spend more time with the children if they had more in common with them. Parents learn so much by being interested in their children's activities and passions. It's part of parenting. It's not common for children to be interested in politics and finance and more adult interests. It's up to a parent to be receptive to their children's ideas and offer a range of activities. They can also take an interest in what happened at school and with friends. It is such a pleasure to be involved in their development.

The vast majority of parents are very dedicated and do their best, despite the way our M-DS is structured. However, if all members of society could make this paradigm shift enabling children to experience FMB, not only would it support parents in being more effective, it would also assist their children (our next generation) to bring peace and abundance to the world and hopefully bring in true democracy, which is discussed in the next chapter.

CHAPTER 9

True Democracy Is Politicians Collaborating with One Another for the Benefit of All

It may sound quaint to some modern cynical ears, but politicians are actually supposed to be serving the people. What has gone wrong? Where is the honesty, transparency, accountability, and integrity? In a true democracy and a political system where the feminine and masculine principles are in balance, we would see politicians collaborating with one another to achieve the best results for the whole population.

POLITICS AND RELIGION

My parents got married when they were very young. My mother was twenty, and my father was twenty-three. I don't think she was particularly religious, but my mother always went to church, almost out of habit, because everyone else did. She thought it was the right thing to do. My father rejected the church as a teenager when, as he told me, "The boys would go to a different church depending on where the good-looking girls were".

He did, on the other hand, go to Australian Labor Party meetings. It was seen as the workers' party. My mother was a bit of a snob and didn't like him going to those meetings, while my father wasn't keen on her going to church. They had some disagreements, then decided if she stopped going to church, he would stop going to Australian Labor Party meetings.

My brother, who is older than me, was christened Presbyterian because he was going to a Presbyterian school. When I was born, my parents planned to send me to an independent school, so I wasn't christened. I never went to church and only had a little religious instruction at school. I think of my childhood as idyllic—free from religion and politics.

What I see now is people who are fed up with politicians bickering and squabbling, behaving in emotionally immature ways. This is fairly inevitable because, as we saw in Chapter 2, emotions that are feminine can be distorted or underdeveloped due to the unbalanced line-up of masculine energies.

So many politicians have lost sight of what politics is all about. Many politicians seem to have the hierarchical belief that they are more important than the general public, when in fact they are supposed to be serving the public. They're supposed to be helping, not in it for what they can get out of it.

HONESTY, TRANSPARENCY, ACCOUNTABILITY, AND INTEGRITY

These are some of the key characteristics we want in our politicians, and they clearly require Feminine Masculine Balance (FMB).

- Honesty is expressing openly what is happening without any defensiveness. This requires a person to be true to themselves and clear about who they are. Honest people stand up for their beliefs and are unafraid to speak their minds but are also open to changing their minds if presented with ideas that ring true. Honest individuals need to be thick-skinned because they may be opposed by others' insecure defensiveness. Honest people can be trusted and generally have better mental and physical health because they don't have to deal with the stress and anxiety of dishonesty—having to remember lies and being found out.

- Transparency in politics is providing the means to openly examine the process of decision making and holding politicians accountable. It is especially important in fighting corruption, which, of course, ties in with the masculine-dominated pattern of greed, control, and domination.

- Accountability is the responsibility and obligation of politicians to act in the best interests of society or face the consequences. They are held responsible for their actions.

- Integrity is the quality of being whole and complete while having the personal qualities of fairness, moral and ethical principles, and soundness of moral character.

These four characteristics require politicians to be **aware** of, and **sensibly** know how to respond to and **integrate**, the various needs of the population in a **discerning, flexible, compassionate, nurturing,** and **collaborative** way, while being **mindfully proactive** of our **interdependence**. We would then be able to **trust** them. In other words: Feminine Masculine Balance.

ADVERSARIAL VERSUS COLLABORATIVE APPROACHES

In Australia, many politicians are trained in law and their training is very **rational**, **logical**, and **analytical**. In spite of some changes, lawyers still tend to operate from an **adversarial**, **competitive** approach. Politicians **compete** to achieve their position within their own party, then the parties **compete** against one another to win.

The adversarial approach is based on the masculine either/or belief that one person is right and the other is wrong. Each adversary is trying to prove they are right beyond a shadow of a doubt. Adversarialists revel in conflict and any perceived weaknesses must be attacked to make the idea stronger. The result is that one person loses and the other wins, and the result is clear. The advantage of this approach is that it forces every idea to be examined via tapping into the motivating power of competition.

Unfortunately, the disadvantages of the adversarial approach are many, particularly for politicians because they belong to a party that stands behind a large range of issues.

- The adversarial approach on an issue can lead to a politician who belongs to a particular political party being opposed to something they actually agree with. This makes it more difficult to be honest and consistent with their point of view. The result is the constituency distrusting them, and then they would find it difficult to get support for decisions in the future.

- Because the adversarial approach is so either/or, it makes it difficult for the politician to see the other side and find any common ground, often delaying the decision-making process.
- It is thrilling for a politician to win an issue but demoralising for those who lose, which, of course, can also have serious consequences for the needs of the general public.
- It is also difficult to have a meaningful discussion, and an adversarial approach can result in irrational decisions.

With the adversarial competitive approach, many Australians seem to back their political party like their sporting teams. As a result of this, they are often incapable of seeing when their party has made a mistake and are unwilling to discuss it. Politicians do this, too—always having to be right and exhibiting a variety of antics to avoid admitting to mistakes. With an adversarial opposition on their backs all the time, they don't want to admit when they are wrong.

PATTERN OF BEHAVIOUR: MOVING TOWARDS DEMOCRACY

Commonly, there are two major parties—the ruling party which is in "power" (dominating and controlling[m]) and the "opposition" (who take the opposite point of view). Many politicians are highly rational[m] and logical,[m] competing[m] to achieve their positions within the party and then competing[m] to win elections. This has resulted in a hierarchical,[m] detached,[m] and competitive[m] system with all the wheeling and dealing, emotionally immature squabbling, and a focus on reelection.

Collaboration[b] allows respect for different ideas, and perhaps we can move away from masculine[m]-dominated rulership towards politicians who are more sensible,[b] aware,[b] and knowing,[b] accepting collaboration[b] as normal mature behaviour and behaving with compassion,[b] flexibility,[b] trust,[b] and discernment[b]; mindful[b] of the needs of the whole community; and collaborating[b] together with honesty, transparency, accountability, and integrity to achieve the best outcome for all.

Note: The superscripts f—feminine, m—masculine, and b—blend refer to the words in the *Blending Some Feminine and Masculine Principles* table.

In a mostly two-party system where there is a "ruling party" and an "opposition" it often seems that the opposition has to automatically oppose whatever is being proposed. Then, if they win the next election, they often don't stick to those opposite points of view.

With the collaborative approach, the participants respect the other people's ideas and are willing to listen to their point of view. Where there is confusion, they ask for further clarification and may restate the idea in their own words to check if they have understood the point being made. In a collaborative discussion, each party builds on the other's good ideas, working together to produce the best result. Collaboration assumes that all participants are working together to help achieve a mutual goal—one that hopefully includes contributions from every participant.

If politicians worked collaboratively, their common goal would always be for the best possible outcome for the general public. The advantages of the collaborative approach are:

- Because everyone is involved in making the final decision, they feel more invested in the result and more motivated to support its implementation.
- There are no losers and, even if some ideas weren't used, they were at least given consideration and time was taken to understand their point of view.
- People work together to create better ideas rather than feel obliged to stick to their own party line.

The disadvantage of the collaborative approach, especially from the point of view of masculine-dominated politicians, is that it isn't competitive. Their egos would not be on the line and ideas may not be criticised as strongly as they would be with the adversarial approach. Given that the urge for politicians to compete and win is primal, and collaboration is less natural for them, they would probably need a lot of practice to develop collaborative habits.

Adversarialists make the argument that someone who discusses both sides of an argument is "sitting on the fence". What better position to have to be able to see both points of view? That is the first step towards achieving a fair resolution.

It is easily seen that collaboration is FMB: it allows for respect for different ideas, with a **sensible awareness** and **knowing** that **collaboration** is normal, mature behaviour. Responding with **compassion, flexibility, trust,** and **discernment allows** one to be **mindful** of the needs of the whole community.

POLITICS IN BALANCE

Often, when we're told something as a tourist, it's not necessarily completely accurate. I like to think this story was:

In 2007, when Bhutan was preparing for their first mock democratic election, the King explained the democratic system and then proceeded to nominate representatives to each party. The King told the representatives to tour the country and tell the people what they would do for their country and later the people would vote for them.

The people's first reaction was to say, "Oh, no, no, we love you, King. We don't want to do that". However, he told them, "But you might have a bad King. We need to have democracy, a constitution, and political parties". So, the representatives went off on their campaigns—working quite happily together with a completely different attitude than the way the rest of the world approaches political campaigns.

I loved the idea, and perhaps it is a window into what a more balanced political system might look like. Now, I'm not saying Bhutanese are never competitive. They love their archery!

MOVING TOWARDS TRUE DEMOCRACY

It is interesting that there seems to be a trend away from the highly competitive two-party system towards a multi-party system, and I'm hoping that that may encourage more collaboration as it becomes increasingly more difficult to have a ruling party.

Rulership implies imposition by a sovereign authority and the obligation of obedience on the part of all subjects to that authority. This is dictatorship, masculine-dominated control and domination. This attitude is echoed by some politicians who think they are superior to the people they serve.

At times, the word *leadership* is used as a term for people who control and dominate others, but true leadership is different. Leaders have *emotional intelligence*, a term that first appeared in a paper by Michael Beldoch and was later popularised by Daniel Goleman in his book of the same name. Emotional intelligence is a balance of feminine and masculine qualities. It is the ability to recognise and manage our own emotions and those of others using emotional awareness and also the ability to harness our emotions while applying them to thinking and problem-solving.

Leaders develop themselves and then use that skill to lead or guide others and assist them in achieving that same skill using the combination of masculine "doing" and feminine "being". A leader doesn't see themselves as superior to the people who have less experience. They understand that they have the responsibility to assist other people to achieve or learn what they themselves have already accomplished.

In politics, leadership comes back to **honesty** and being open about the decision-making process, **transparency**, **accountability** for their **actions**, being **sensitive** to the needs of the general public, and doing it all with **integrity**.

I know there are politicians doing wonderful work behind the scenes, but this is undermined by their behaviour in parliament and the adversarial, masculine-dominated political culture. Politicians who think they can change the world to make it a better place through a masculine-dominated approach are misguided. It has already been shown in this and Chapters 3 and 7 that, without an FMB approach, war is inevitable, greed and poverty are inevitable, and the general population has difficulty trusting politicians because of their adversarial behaviour.

When politicians and the people with whom they work can make the paradigm shift to FMB, then we shall see true democracy.

In the next chapter, we move on to religion.

CHAPTER 10

Religion Was Set Up by Men, for Men

When I was fifteen, my very wise English teacher told the class that religious people aren't necessarily spiritual, and spiritual people aren't necessarily religious. As I mentioned in the last chapter, I had a little religious teaching at school and none at home. I never went to church, and God was never mentioned. Our family was completely unreligious.

I had an interesting experience when I was nine years old. At that age, we would gauge ourselves as "good" or "bad" by whether or not someone was naughty in class. I was a cooperative child, but we all knew who the naughtiest girl in class was. When she heard that I didn't go to church, she told me I was "bad" and I remember thinking, "This church business can't be much if they say the naughtiest girl in class is good and I, one of the *good* children in the class, am bad".

This was one of many experiences that shaped my understanding of religion, and later I had experiences that shaped my understanding of spirituality.

PHYSICAL AND NONPHYSICAL

Living in a tangible, physical world, we tend to identify ourselves as our body, without reflecting much on what else there is. I had heard of reincarnation and spirits, but I never really thought about it until my first baby, Marcus, died of cot death. When I realised there was something wrong, I picked him up, and in that moment, I felt the nonphysical aspect of him melt away. With his lifeless body in my arms, I felt what some would call his spirit hovering above him. I then realised that if we observe the dead body of someone we have known, the person isn't there; it's lifeless. Some people refer to the body as "the temple of the soul". It seems to me that we have a physical aspect, the body, and a nonphysical or spiritual aspect, and they operate differently. The body dies and the nonphysical leaves the body and withdraws. It's my belief that the nonphysical is ageless and has no gender. Old people don't usually feel as old as their bodies, and I think gender only exists on the Earth plane.

The hierarchical Masculine-Dominated Society (M-DS) thinks in order of superiority: him, her, it. *It*, having no gender, is a derogative term. However, in a Feminine Masculine Balanced (FMB) society, these three pronouns would be considered as different, not superior nor inferior to one another. *God* is a masculine term and, when we adopt FMB, this term would no longer be used to show disrespect for the feminine. Instead, another word would be found to reflect that it has no gender.

The nonphysical operates in a different way than the physical world. The process of proof, which is so important on the Earth plane, does not exist. The nonphysical is ubiquitous, including animals, plants, and the earth. It is far more extensive than purely a male entity.

THE DEVELOPMENT OF RELIGION

The bases of all religions are similar but with differing procedures and rituals. They were set up and evolved to teach people to live peaceful, good, caring, ethical, responsible lives. Unfortunately, they were set up in an M-DS with hierarchy, domination, and control—particularly control of women.

In Chapter 2 it was observed that patrilineal inheritance led men to control women's sexuality and, therefore, their lives. Those who developed religions took advantage of this concept and produced texts such as the Torah, Bible, and Quran, which preach discrimination against women, degradation and subjugation of women, and even violence against women! They teach that women are not only inferior but also must obey men because their male God tells us men are their masters.

A classic example of religion being masculine-dominated is the story of Adam and Eve. In the garden of Eden, Eve plucked the apple from the Tree of Knowledge and offered it to Adam. He didn't have to accept it. He made a choice. When things went wrong, instead of *taking responsibility for his decision* Adam blamed Eve (emotional immaturity). This pattern of behaviour still continues with masculine-dominated people today. If anything goes wrong in their life, they blame someone else rather than taking responsibility for their own decisions. Now perhaps Eve was to blame, but I once read a comment by a feminist author that stated that even if Eve—and therefore all women— were guilty, surely after 2,000 years we've done our time! Where is the religious compassion and forgiveness?

Having learned about psychological projection, I realised that man created God rather than the other way around. Psychological projection is a defence mechanism people subconsciously use to cope with feelings and emotions that we have trouble expressing or coming to terms with. Clearly, the mysteries of life are particularly challenging, and all cultures and societies have developed belief systems to explain them. In the case of most Masculine-Dominated Societies, a male god was chosen. This idea is not new. An article in *Art & Pop Culture* about man's invention of God as a masculine entity being a Psychological Projection states that "A prominent precursor in the formulation of the projection principle was Giambattista Vico (23 June 1668–23 January 1744), and an early formulation of it is found in ancient Greek writer Xenophanes (c.c. 570–c. 475 BC), who observed that 'the gods of Ethiopians were inevitably black with flat noses while those of the Thracians were blond with blue eyes'. In 1841, Ludwig Feuerbach (July 28, 1804–September 13, 1872), was the first to employ this concept as the basis for a systematic critique of religion[14]".

HIERARCHY AND IMBALANCE

The feminine allows others to control their own lives and the masculine requires controlling one's own life. The blend of the two is **trust**. Religions show a lack of trust in people to take responsibility for their own lives, have integrity, and be peaceful, good, and caring. FMB leadership and guidance is welcome but masculine-dominated dogma is not. We are all fallible human beings, but so much of the wrongdoing in society comes from the imbal-

---

14   "Psychological Projection", *Art & Pop Culture*, accessed May 21, 2018, http://www.artandpopularculture.com/Psychological_projection.

ance of the feminine and masculine, as we have seen in the previous chapters.

Religious followers are equally fallible, which has become even more evident with the cover-ups of widespread paedophilia in masculine-dominated institutions, including religious institutions—a clear sign of imbalance. The cover-ups show an extraordinary lack of integrity, awareness, and compassion. It is very distressing that honesty, compassion, and joy are preached by religious leaders, when at the same time paedophilia causes untold damage to human lives.

The lack of understanding towards the lesbian, gay, bisexual, transgender, gender diverse, intersex, and queer (LGBTIQ+) communities also shows the conditional nature of the qualities such as love, hope, joy, wisdom, humility, and generosity preached by religions. To narrowly and rigidly define marriage to suit a particular group, and not only deny anyone who is different to be married but try to impose it on the whole society, is a sad reflection of how far from core values religions have travelled.

PATTERN OF BEHAVIOUR: MARRIAGE EQUALITY

Religions say that marriage is only between a man and a woman. That is fine, but why impose your beliefs on people who are not religious?

If we analyse this in terms of the table, this is a very rational,[m] logical[m] argument and rather narrow and divisive.[m] Those who believe in marriage equality combine their intuition,[f] emotional[f] nature, and imagination[f] with their rational,[m] logical,[m] analytical[m] nature to have an integrated[b] sensible[b] awareness[b] and knowing[b] attitude towards LGBTIQ people. Combining detachment[m] and sensitivity,[f] they compassionately[b] recognise LGBTIQ people's need to express their love and commitment to one another and also allow[f] them to have the same legal rights associated with marriage, such as taxes, property ownership, inheritance, adoption, and next-of-kin recognition. This is an issue of trust.[b]

Note: The superscripts f—feminine, m—masculine, and b—blend refer to the words in the *Blending Some Feminine and Masculine Principles* table.

Although people discuss a variety of reasons why, "It is more blessed to give than receive" (Acts 20:35), when you think about it, it is a masculine hierarchical attempt to diminish the feminine because giving is masculine and receiving is feminine. It was pointed out in Chapter 7 that for someone to give, someone else has to receive and, in that sense, they are doing the other person a favour by being willing to receive. Some people turn this into a domination and control issue: "I am more important than you because I'm giving to you". This can disempower and diminish the receiver, leaving some people feeling uncomfortable and reluctant to receive.

It is confusing to hear leaders of masculine-dominated religions calling for "world peace" when they offend roughly 50 percent of the population by having religious texts which preach discrimination, degradation, subjugation, and even violence against women. As was discussed in Chapters 2 and 3, violence is a result of Feminine Masculine Imbalance due to masculine domination or a distortion of masculine energies and, therefore, damaged feminine energies. As religious beliefs are so pervasive, it is important that religious leaders take FMB seriously. Just as Adam should have taken responsibility for his decision in the Garden of Eden, church leaders now need to take responsibility for their religions' histories of oppression of women and, therefore, the feminine. It is time to revise religious texts to heal past injustices, which will not only benefit women but will consequently heal men as well. We can then move on to a future that values and respects women and, therefore, the feminine. A future of FMB. Only then can church leaders genuinely call for world peace.

REPRODUCTIVE OPPRESSION

Religions often encourage women to have many children (**quantity**) rather than opting for fewer children and having more **quality** of life. Some parents are exceptionally capable at caring for a larger number of children but for most, having two to four children is quite enough and allows the parents to give their children the most valuable thing a parent has to offer: time. Having a large number of babies was more appropriate in an agrarian society and at a time when there were high infant and child mortality rates, but now it is not advisable, particularly considering the Earth has a massive population problem. Also, as mentioned in Chapter 2, women are not weak or helpless but are significantly incapacitated for a few months before birth, and then nursing the baby and recovering from childbirth. That's when they need protection, and the more children they have, the more they are vulnerable to domination and control by men. The line-up of masculine energies without the balance of the feminine took advantage of this and distorted the need for protection into domination and control. Added to that, having large families exacerbates the cycle of poverty—a way to control people. The more children a woman bears, the more followers of a religion—an added benefit to the masculine competitive nature of religions. Yet again, it's quantity rather than quality.

END-OF-LIFE COMPASSION

As I discussed in Chapter 5, before my parents died, they suffered more than any person should. Surveys have shown that the main opposition to dying with dignity comes from religions. Perhaps one of the problems is that, from a masculine perspective, life is seen as a straight line: beginning, middle, and end. That's it. However, the feminine is a circle: birth, growth, culmination, decay, death, birth, growth, culmination, etc. It's the natural cycle of life. Blending the two into a spiral shows each life cycle. Perhaps that is part of the problem—the belief that we only have one life. This can result in a fear of death and there being nothing thereafter. Even if one doesn't believe that we have more than one life (recycling), the understanding of cycles can give a person more acceptance of the cycle of life and death. Also, straight-line thinking detaches from showing common sense, discernment and having compassion for suffering.

PATTERN OF BEHAVIOUR: DYING WITH DIGNITY

Religions say that euthanasia is against the word and will of God. Yes, but I wonder what the Goddess' word and will are? Combining the feminine and masculine, that is, intuition,[f] emotional[f] nature, and imagination[f] with the rational,[m] logical,[m] and analytical,[m] we can achieve an integrated,[b] sensible,[b] persuasive,[b] and educated[b] approach to the sanctity of life. Being able to see other people's points of view (holistic[f] approach), although they may not necessarily agree with them, would allow the ability to reflect[f] on the anguish of a person who is suffering from extreme pain/end of life frailty and would lead to compassion[b] (combination of detachment[m] and sensitivity[f]) for that person.

Decision-makers would not only value quantity[m] of life but also have the discernment[b] to know that quality[f] of life is also important and therefore allow people to control their own lives.[f] Some detached[m] people say that suffering may have value. I guess it is a matter of degree, and that is where sensitivity[f] and discernment[b] come in. Clearly, euthanasia must have strict guidelines, and only a very controlling[m] M-DS would move towards killing people who are thought to be undesirable.

Note: The superscripts f—feminine, m—masculine, and b—blend refer to the words in the *Blending Some Feminine and Masculine Principles* table.

MOVING TOWARDS BALANCE IN RELIGION

There is no doubt that religions and religious people do many good things, and nonreligious people do, too. However, being set up by men for men, religions are basically masculine-dominated corporations. My father used to play tennis with a priest and would tease the priest about this sentiment. He didn't deny it.

One of the main values in following a religion is the traditions it offers. Tradition is important to religious people and also nonreligious people. Tradition reinforces values such as freedom, faith, integrity, a good education, personal responsibility, ethics, and the value of being selfless. It also provides a forum to showcase role models and celebrate the things that really matter in life. Tradition contributes a sense of comfort and belonging, can bring families together, and enables people to reconnect with friends. It serves as an avenue for creating lasting memories. Importantly, traditions offer an excellent context for meaningful pause and reflection and, if they are ignored, we're in danger of damaging the underpinning of our identity.

However, religions do not have a monopoly on traditions, and it is important to examine all of them to determine if they are in FMB. Leaders, role models, and parents need to work towards every opportunity available to reinforce balanced values and beliefs, and to prevent taking these values for granted so that our beliefs can evolve into providing us with a peaceful and abundant society.

As long as religions retain their unrevised, un-modernized religious texts, balance won't be possible. Until they allow women, representing the feminine, to be equally involved in all areas of the religion, they won't achieve balance. Masculine domination and control clearly don't work, so isn't it time to try something else? Long term, this could be possible, but there's so much resistance to change. I wonder if this is one of the reasons why some more advanced communities are becoming more secular. Will it ever be possible for religions to change?

In the following chapter, we shall see how the introduction of monotheistic religions is the basis of the change in the concept of power.

CHAPTER 11

True Power Is Being Able to Control Our Own Lives...Not Controlling and Dominating Others

True power comes from Feminine Masculine Balance (FMB) within and has nothing to do with dominating and controlling others.

Over the years, I've experienced emotionally abusive relationships and observed the way dominating men and women behave, creating unpleasant consequences from those interactions. Though I didn't feel that control from my father and brother, who weren't particularly sexist, I did have a dominating, controlling mother. She had a narcissistic personality disorder, so everything had to go her way. Later in life, because I hadn't dealt with that during my upbringing, I attracted that in some of my other relationships.

TWO KINDS OF POWER AND THE CONTINUUM

Journalists and others refer to some people as "powerful" when, in fact, they are dominating and controlling. There are various usages of the word *power*, and this type of power is *power over* other people, other animals, things, and the environment, as we have seen in previous chapters. People who believe in power-over expect to get what they want through domination and control at any cost. They generally make no distinction between right and wrong, and they like to expand their influence. Power-over kills the spirit.

On the other hand, true power is the ability to relate to and be aware of other people, animals, and the environment with an understanding of our interdependence and a concern for the welfare of all. It nourishes the spirit. I used to use the term *personal power* but, on checking the internet, masculine-dominated businesspeople use this term to describe influencing people to do what they want them to do, and I guess it is a softer way of controlling people. I therefore use the term *true power* but was amused when I checked on the internet and there were references to electricity! As with other aspects of human behaviour, there is a continuum between one end of the polarity and the other.

Historically, the emergence of power-over occurred concurrently with that of Masculine-Dominated Societies. In this book's introduction, I mentioned societies in the Neolithic period that were female-centred, not female-ruled. They interacted with nature, understanding that, to a certain extent, they could influence it but were also influenced *by* it—thunderstorms, floods, fires, etc. As a result, they developed the concept of power as an interplay between different elements and modelled their society on this. Understanding interdependence, they didn't see any member of the community as superior to another because they respected each individual's particular contribution. Even elders of the tribe recognised that they needed support from other members of the community in the same way that the members of the community needed guidance from them. In other words, they were each operating from a position of true power.

With the introduction of the concept of a Supreme Male God, a single spirit that is omnipotently ruling over the world and its people and judging them for their sins, the concept of domination and control was born. Some people claimed to be able to communicate with this God, and they were genuinely wanting to help people live peaceful, good, caring, ethical, and responsible lives. However, others setting up religions interpreted this as an opportunity to separate themselves from the rest of the community, thus introducing the concept of hierarchy. From this concept of hierarchy, exclusive classes developed, who believed they must rule over everyone else.

Dictatorships, wars, state rulership struggles, and building of empires were results of this new paradigm. With the later development of science and technology, a new kind of "religion" evolved, dominating and controlling nature and its people in a different way. Science and technology have been in conflict with religion ever since. However, controlling nature doesn't always work. For example, floods can wash away buildings, bridges, and dams. In the same way, dictatorships and aristocracies don't work in the long term because they depend on submission and agreement of their citizens.

ADDICTION TO POWER-OVER

In his brilliant TED talk on "The Power of Addiction and Addiction to Power", Gabor Maté, specialist in terminal diseases, chemical dependents, and HIV-positive patients, informs us that addicts feel empty, want to escape from their own minds, and try to alleviate these feelings with addictive substances. The cause of this is childhood experiences—something they didn't get when they were young. Maté encourages us to understand their suffering and why they seek relief. He compares the drug addict injecting substances into their bodies to the rest of the population injecting chemicals into the planet, the atmosphere, the oceans, and the environment, and asks the question: What does the greatest harm—consumerism and oil or individuals taking drugs?

By studying people who were addicted to power-over and acquisition of wealth, he noticed that they were outsiders and felt insecure and inferior. To alleviate those feelings, they needed power over others and, in order to get and maintain that power, they were willing to fight wars and even kill.

Maté further compares those who are addicted to power with Buddha and Jesus. Both men were tempted by the devil, and one thing he offered was power over others. They both refused because they had the power within themselves and didn't need it from the outside. They didn't want to control people; they wanted to teach people by example, kindness, and wisdom, not through force. Jesus' response to this was, "The Kingdom of God is within". As Buddha lay dying he said, "Don't mourn me and don't worship me. Find the lamp inside yourself, be a lamp unto yourselves, find a light within[15]". In other words, they both had true power.

Maté points out that because addiction to power is always about emptiness, people in power are trying to fill that void from the outside. We can't expect them to help with the loss of environment, global warming, and depredation of the oceans because the people in power are very often some of the emptiest people in the world. We need to find that light within ourselves, our own wisdom and creativity to improve ourselves, our communities, and the environment.

He also talks about how some say human nature is competitive, aggressive, and selfish (masculine-dominated behaviour). He believes the opposite: that human nature is cooperative, generous, and community-minded (FMB), and he gives the example of the TED conferences, where people share information and are committed to a better world.

TRUE POWER

Apart from Buddha and Jesus, another example of true power is a performer such as an actress, actor, or dancer

---

15   Gabor Maté, "The Power of Addiction and The Addiction of Power: Gabor Maté at TEDxRio+20", YouTube video, 18:46, October 9, 2012, https://www.youtube.com/watch?v=66cYcSak6nE.

who has stage presence. Stage presence is being in the present or being mindful—a blend of being and doing. Stage presence draws us in and commands our full attention. The charisma is inspiring and we feel excited by it. The artist uses their sensitivity, intuition, and imagination to portray their role. They are in control of their performance, and are stimulating and uplifting the audience without trying to control or dominate them.

True power includes self-awareness, accepting ourselves just as we are, making conscious choices, and being committed to what we believe in and what is important to us. True power is being willing to promote growth and well-being not only for ourselves, but for others as well. It is also enjoying participating in life, not only to achieve our own goals, but assisting others to also achieve their goals. True power is rejoicing in the richness and diversity of life.

PATTERN OF BEHAVIOUR: POWER-OVER

Power over others comes from a detached,[m] rational,[m] logical,[m] hierarchical[m] *lack* of understanding that we are all interdependent.[b] There is an insecure (*lack* of trust[b]) need to not only control one's own life[m] but control and dominate others as well—straight-line thinking.[m] A person who expresses power-over acts in a defensive,[m] strong,[m] independent,[m] and competitive[m] manner to maintain their fantasy of being superior to others. If this person were able to see another point of view (holistic[f] thinking) and had the sensitivity,[f] intuition,[f] and imagination[f] to trust[b] others to control their own lives,[f] she/he would have the sense,[b] awareness,[b] and knowing[b] to recognise that we are all interdependent.[b]

Note: The superscripts f—feminine, m—masculine, and b—blend refer to the words in the *Blending Some Feminine and Masculine Principles* table.

THE POWER OF LANGUAGE

Words are powerful, and they can be dominating and controlling in themselves. Journalists, corporations, and people who have a huge impact on society need to change their thinking and the way they use their words. Acknowledge that a so-called powerful person is actually dominating and controlling. Acknowledge that this kind of power is not a good thing—it's belittling, demeaning, and disempowering. Our language needs to shift to reflect true power.

Feminine words need to be respected in the same way, not used as derogatory terms. In the introduction, I mention that Dale Spender writes about how the feminine is denigrated through language. That was in 1980, and nothing has changed! A good deal of work has to be done to reform our language to achieve FMB.

MOVING TOWARDS CHOOSING TRUE POWER

At this point in our history we have a clear choice. We can continue on our path of control and domination of other people, animals, plants, the Earth, oceans, and atmosphere, or we can integrate our feminine and masculine energies to recognise that we are **interdependent**. We can develop into truly powerful, **sensible, aware, trustworthy, knowing** human **beings mindfully, proactively,** and **collaboratively nurturing** each other and the planet by **responding** with **compassion, flexibility,** and **discernment**. With this paradigm shift, peace, abundance, and a healthy planet are possible.

Conclusion

HEALING THE FEMININE, HEALING THE MASCULINE

To heal is to make things whole. As we heal the feminine energies by valuing, respecting and utilising them to the same degree as the masculine energies, the masculine energies will also heal, achieving Feminine Masculine Balance (FMB).

As a consequence:

- Young men will no longer think they have to be the opposite of their mothers, and young women will learn about the balanced masculine from their fathers.
- Young men won't be stuck in the "Man Box", where they internalise and agree with society's rigid mes-

sages on how a man should behave, and neither women nor men will be stuck in claustrophobic stereotypes, so they can be true to themselves.

- Domestic violence will be a thing of the past.
- Disagreements will be negotiated peacefully.
- We will take responsibility for healing the planet.
- We will integrate medicine with healing practices.
- We will understand that we need a balance between activities (work and play) and stillness (sleep and meditation, etc.).
- We shall rejoice in abundance and diversity.
- Parents will collaborate with one another in assisting their children to reach their full potential on all levels of their being.
- Politicians will collaborate with one another, leading to true democracy.
- Religions (particularly religious texts) will be revised to be relevant to all genders and the modern world.
- We will choose true power instead of power-over.

And these are only some examples of the many changes that will occur.

Delightfully and unfortunately, we are very complex beings—delightfully because it provides richness and diversity in life, and unfortunately because achieving FMB isn't easy, particularly because masculine domination has been so ingrained in our society for millennia. Although the tide is turning and we're beginning to achieve a balance, there's still a long way to go in every aspect of our lives. Virtually every minute of the day, we could be mindfully making little shifts here and there towards balance.

MOVING TOWARDS FEMININE MASCULINE BALANCE THROUGH AWARENESS

When I say the masculine and feminine need to be in balance, I'm not talking about them being equal in expression at all times. The pendulum will swing from one side to the other, but we do need to express any energy backed up by the other side. It's a matter of what is appropriate in the situation. The goal is homeostasis. In the body, we see the same sort of effort to return to the centre, in the sense that it's not necessarily being *in* balance at all times, but it's working *towards* balance at all times. There is a continuum between each end of the polarities. There needs to be equal acknowledgment and respect for all the energies.

In her book *Pioneering the Possible*[16], Scilla Elworthy has written beautiful descriptions of the deep feminine and the deep masculine. In terms of FMB, the deep feminine is the expression of feminine energies backed up by the masculine, and similarly, the deep masculine is the expres-

---

16   Scilla Elworthy, *Pioneering the Possible. Awakened Leadership for a World That Works* (California: North Atlantic Books, 2014), 36-37.

sion of masculine energies backed up by the feminine. In that sense, they are balanced.

I also want to clarify that all of the energies in the *Blending Some Feminine and Masculine Principles* table are neutral in themselves. They are not "good" or "bad". For example, in Chapter 2, anger is mentioned, and there are examples of constructive and destructive anger. Anger is a useful tool that lets us know that things aren't the way we want them to be and is also a fuel to assist us to act to fix the problem. It is meant to be acted upon (constructive anger) not acted out (destructive anger).

In addition, throughout the book, there have been many references to competition and competitive behaviour. Again, competition itself is not "good" or "bad"—it can be healthy or unhealthy depending on the circumstances and how it is lined up with other masculine and feminine energies. Let's take sport for example. Cheating to win at all costs is clearly unhealthy competition. However, most teams compete in a healthy way but, interestingly, champion sports people have to be competitive *and* collaborative (a blend of the feminine and masculine). Yes, a team is competing against another team but there is a saying: "A champion team is more effective than a team of champions". In other words, if there is a team of very skilled players but they are not collaborating with one another, they do not get the best results, compared to a team who does collaborate. Any team also needs to collaborate with its coach. In the case of individual sports, a player still needs to collaborate with the coach.

To all masculine-dominated people who feel challenged by these ideas, please don't throw the baby out with the bath water, but make the effort to consider making the paradigm shift. You are really quite safe because I am not recommending lessening the importance of masculine energies but just bringing the feminine energies up to the same value and respect as the masculine energies. As this happens, the world may feel more feminine than masculine, when it is actually in balance but more feminine than it was before.

A small experiment can clarify this: Take three bowls of water—one with tolerably hot water, one with warm water, and one with tolerably cold water. Put your right hand into the cold water and your left hand into the hot water and let your hands come to the temperature of the water they are in. If you then plunge your hands into the warm water, the right hand that's been cold will feel the warm water as being hotter than the left hand that has been in the hot water.

In Chapter 8, it was mentioned that in the 1960s women chose to go out to paid employment, resulting in men taking a greater interest in assisting with parenting. I see this as a step towards greater FMB. As the feminine is healed, the masculine will be healed as a consequence. I am also hoping that FMB is introduced and practised in schools, not only to assist our future generation, but it will also result in children bringing these concepts home and passing them on to their parents. It is an effective way to shift adult attitudes in our society.

USING THE TABLE

The table of *Blending Some Feminine and Masculine Principles* can be a constant reference in our own lives, homes, workplaces, and organizations. We can also use it when thinking about our language and behaviour. For example, people who suffer from anger and violent outbursts can work towards including feminine energies on the left-hand side of the table and refer back to the patterns of violence in Chapters 2 and 3.

Another example might be when a friend has a tragedy. It can be difficult to help them. We need to be a little detached in order to be compassionate so that we are not too sensitive to their sadness about their tragedy. We need to step back and feel slight detachment alongside sensitivity; that's where compassion lies.

FINAL WORDS

Combining the feminine as a circle and the masculine as a straight line produces a spiral. I consider this book is the first cycle of a spiral towards a better world. This book is a teaser to get people to think and therefore act in different ways.

I have written how the FMB can operate in different "worlds"—for example, medicine and religion from the point of view of an outsider, and I invite people who are inside these worlds to pursue and integrate these ideas with their inside knowledge.

There are many fields of interest and "worlds" within this world: political, sporting, artistic, academic, legal, journalistic...I invite people who are intimately familiar with these "worlds" to develop this FMB concept in relation to their experience to hopefully make their "world" more balanced. Imagine how the world could shift if everyone applied this FMB lens to their own field of endeavour! If leaders find it is difficult to attract women (representing the feminine) to their field of endeavour, maybe it is because their masculine-dominated culture is not attractive, and perhaps they need reach out for help to make it more appealing.

Awareness is the first step to effect change, and developing that awareness is the intention of this book. If we initially make the change step by step within ourselves, as individuals, it can then ripple out to family, friends, and the community at large.

I hope this book has helped people wake up to the thing that lies beneath the major problems in our supposedly advanced civilised age—that is the lack of Feminine Masculine Balance. Can we, as a society, make this paradigm shift?

Acknowledgments

The culmination of years of experience and observation is the basis of this book, and to all the people who have been in my life, to all writers, teachers, family and friends, plays, talks, radio, and TV too numerous to name, who shaped these experiences and observations, I thank you all.

Without the people from Book in A Box—Zach Obront, Kate Rallis, Mark Chait, Nikki Katz, Anton Khodakovsky, and Michael Nagin—this book would never have happened. Thank you for your open minds, enthusiasm, friendliness, encouragement, and amazing technical abilities. Also, thank you to the people who have produced all the wonderful technology we have today, especially cut and paste! I remember the days when we had to literally cut the paper and sticky tape it together when writing our developing theses!

There are some I would like to especially mention and thank:

Those who inspired and supported me though the writing journey: Meg Debski, Merryl Key, Tricia Peters, John Burke, Darren Walsh, Anne Ryan, and Mary Rose.

The late Roderick Kidston provided me with his wisdom, inspiration, and insight to guide me to having the courage to complete this book.

The late Cousin Bill (Bill Middleton), from whom I received the unexpected inheritance, which funded this book.

Kay Jones, wordsmith extraordinaire, who assisted me with just the right words for the table and also for being such a great mentor over the years.

Jacquie Wise who, when I said that I wasn't a writer, told me that we are talking about information here, not literature. For that and other helpful advice, I thank you.

To the many people who supported/helped me in having a joyful life:

Particularly the many years of friendship from Di Osborne, Annie Cantwell, Helen Watters, Jo Pittendrigh, Ann

Goodrich, Barb Thorp, Kath Basjar, Robyn Mathews, and Claire Day.

To my parents, Ted and Jessie, I give thanks for the gift of life and dedicated parenting from which I learned so much, and to my brother, Jamie, for a shared childhood.

Most especially, my reason for being, my children, Matthew and Johanna, their partners, Maria and Josh, and gorgeous grandchildren, Romeo and Cassandra, whose futures, I hope, will be better because of this book. Without them, my life would not have such richness and meaning.

BLENDING SOME FEMININE AND MASCULINE PRINCIPLES

FEMININE	BALANCE	MASCULINE
Cyclical	Spiral	Linear
Intuitive	Sensible	Rational
Emotional	Aware	Logical
Imaginative/Poetic	Knowing	Analytical/"Intellectual"
Holistic/Inclusive	Integrative	Hierarchical/Divisive
Reflective	Proactive	Reactive
Providing/Sustaining	Nurturing	Protective/Defensive
Amenable	Collaborative	Competitive
Dependent	Interdependent	Independent
Being—In the flow	Mindfulness/ Coherence—In action	Doing—Action-orientated
Sensitive	Compassionate	Detached (Indifferent)
Weak	Flexible	Strong
Allowing others to control their own lives	Trusting	Controlling one's own life
Receptive (Receiving)	Responsive	Outgoing (Giving)
(Produces) Quality	Discerning	(Produces) Quantity

About the Author

Jacqueline Mcleod was a health professional and clinician until her lifelong passion for self-development led her to the studies of tarot, astrology, spirituality, and alternative health. Her life purpose is to assist in achieving a balanced society by empowering the feminine in both women and men. With an ongoing interest in painting and creativity, Jacqueline owns a studio and learning space overlooking a beautiful garden in Sandringham, Melbourne, Australia. Her greatest joys are her two adult children and two grandchildren.

Made in the USA
Las Vegas, NV
13 July 2023

74694121R00111